Answering Jehovah's Witnesses

JASON EVERT

Answering
Jehovah's Witnesses

CATHOLIC ANSWERS
SAN DIEGO
2001

Unless otherwise noted, Scipture quotations are taken from the *New World Translation of the Holy Scriptures* (NWT) © 1961, 1981, 1984, Watchtower Bible and Tract Society and International Bible Students Association.

Published by Catholic Answers, Inc.
2020 Gillespie Way
El Cajon, CA 92020
(888) 291-8000 (orders)
(619) 387-0042 (fax)
www.catholic.com (web)
Cover design by Dan Kray, Kray Marketing
Printed in the United States of America
ISBN 1-888992-21-2

For Mary

Acknowledgments

My favorite priest used to recommend that no one pray for patience. He said that the Lord would not give us patience, just opportunities to practice it.

If that is indeed how God works, then James Akin, Trask Tapperson, and Joel Peters must have finished a novena for patience just before I brought them this manuscript. I owe them, especially James, a great debt of thanks for their patient perseverance in bringing this book to completion. As a gift to them, I ask all who read this book to pause and offer a prayer for James, Trask, and Joel.

Contents

PART ONE: INSIDE THE WATCHTOWER

PART TWO: ANSWERING THE WATCHTOWER

Foreword

It's Saturday afternoon, and you're at home spending time getting caught up on some of your chores when the doorbell rings. You open the front door and see two neatly-dressed people standing on your doorstep, their briefcases brimming with the latest issues of *The Watchtower* and *Awake!* They tell you that they are in the neighborhood, talking with people who are concerned about what is happening in the world today—crime, drugs, immorality, violence—and they want a few minutes of your time to share a message with you.

After getting you to agree that humanity is not exactly a paradigm of virtue these days, they appeal to your desire for "a better world" by describing an earth without war, without sickness, without hatred, and without want or need. Then they pique your curiosity by asking you if you would like to know more about such an existence, adding that God's plan for humanity is precisely such a paradise. Since their message in some way seems relevant and since through common courtesy you give them the benefit of the doubt, you agree to listen to what they have to say.

This situation has been played out countless times across most neighborhoods, and it is the proverbial foot-in-the-door approach that can result in unsuspecting Catholics abandoning their religious upbringing to become Jehovah's Witnesses, members of the Watchtower organization. When such a change happens, very often family members and loved ones are left reeling—at a loss to know how to counter the Watchtower's beliefs or how to rescue their loved ones from the spiritual blindness that has enveloped them.

This type of occurrence is real, and its relevance hits home for many Catholics who have brothers, sisters, cousins, grandparents, spouses, or friends "serving Jehovah God." They distribute the Watchtower's publications and warn people of the imminence of Armageddon—the final conflict between God and Satan—the

Watchtower's central theme. In fact, a significant percentage of Jehovah's Witnesses are former Catholics, so this issue cannot be lightly brushed aside by those who profess the One, Holy, Catholic, and Apostolic Faith. The salvation of souls is at stake, and we must do what we can to help those who have been ensnared by the Watchtower.

The reasons people become involved in groups like the Jehovah's Witnesses vary, but they often boil down to three:

- People have been poorly taught the Catholic faith and therefore cannot adequately respond to the Watchtower's theological assault on it. Since the Witnesses are well trained in presenting their beliefs and "proving" them with well-worn Bible verses (which, by the way, are taken out of context), they provide what may at first appear to be compelling reasons to join them. People who are unfamiliar with these doctrinal issues are often easily swayed.

- People experience a void in their lives, such as a desire for love and attention or a quest for purpose and meaning, and they are looking for something to fill that void. Consequently, they turn to groups that offer both companionship and ready-made answers to all of life's most difficult questions.

- People are at transitional periods in their lives (starting college, beginning a new job, undergoing a relocation), and the accompanying disorientation leaves them more susceptible to the influence of groups such as the Witnesses. Once individuals become Jehovah's Witnesses, they are taught to view the Catholic faith as a satanic corruption of the true faith from which they should remove themselves as far as possible.

What, then, is a Catholic to do about a family member or friend who has become a Witness?

Fortunately, there is hope. There are ways to deal with this type of situation, and there are responses to the belief system of the Watchtower organization. We need not plead ignorance or incompetence regarding the subject matter, for with a little education and lots of prayer we can become the very instruments by which the Holy Spirit will lead a person out of the Watchtower's darkness.

One of the best approaches is to know the competition, and in this regard Jason Evert's book will prove to be a useful tool in combating the Jehovah's Witnesses' mind-set and doctrines. Since this work is intended for the "average Catholic," who has no formal training in theology, it is designed to be easily understood and practical.

Beginning with the foundations of the Watchtower organization, the author deals with its presidents and history, moves next through the basic structure and content of the Jehovah's Witnesses' world, and then discusses the various doctrines of the Watchtower and how to refute them. Particular attention is given to some of the favorite verses and standard topics that a Witness will typically use in rejecting the Catholic faith. Finally, some extremely helpful and practical suggestions are offered for how to interact with someone who has become a Jehovah's Witness.

There are some good resources generally available for use in refuting the Watchtower's theology. But very few of them proceed from a specifically Catholic perspective, so invariably such resources are helpful only to a point. Catholics need not be at a disadvantage, however. Since this book is written by a staff apologist at Catholic Answers, the reader can rest assured that its contents are faithful to the Church's teachings.

It is time that Catholics begin to reclaim the spiritual ground lost to the Watchtower organization, and with the help of this book, I am confident that this goal is well within our reach.

—Joel S. Peters
Author, teacher,
and authority on
Jehovah's Witnesses
Mahwah, New Jersey

Reference Information

1) All Bible quotations are taken from the Jehovah's Witnesses' *New World Translation of the Holy Scriptures* (NWT), unless otherwise noted. Other translations used in this work include the *Kingdom Interlinear Translation of the Greek Scriptures* (KIT [Brooklyn: The New World Translation Committee, Watchtower Bible and Tract Society of New York, Inc., 1985]), the *New American Bible* (NAB) and the *Revised Standard Version: Catholic Edition* (RSV:CE).

2) "The Watchtower" (without italics) refers to the Watchtower Bible and Tract Society of New York, Inc., the parent organization of the Jehovah's Witnesses, while *The Watchtower* (in italics) refers to the principal periodical of the Watchtower Bible and Tract Society.

3) *The Watchtower* magazine has been known by several names throughout its history, indicated as follows. Any citations from the magazine dating from 1931 onward will be abbreviated as *The Watchtower*. Other abbreviations used are in parentheses.

> 1879 *Zion's Watch Tower and Herald of Christ's Presence* (*Zion's Watch Tower*)
> 1909 *The Watch Tower and Herald of Christ's Presence* (*The Watch Tower*)
> 1931 *The Watchtower and Herald of Christ's Presence*
> 1939 (January) *The Watchtower and Herald of Christ's Kingdom*
> 1939 (March) *The Watchtower Announcing Jehovah's Kingdom* (it remains this way to date)

4) Some of Charles Taze Russell's followers reprinted *The Watchtower* magazine for the time frame of 1879 (its inception) to 1916 (the year of Russell's death). These bound volumes are called *Watchtower Reprints*. Excerpts from *Zion's Watch Tower* and *The Watch Tower* cited in this book are taken from them. For clarity's sake, the references will include the original date of publication and the original page number(s) in parentheses.

Introduction

Within a few miles of your neighborhood is a Kingdom Hall, the place of worship and instruction for Jehovah's Witnesses. On a wall inside that building is a map. Your house is on it. Your city has been divided up into "field territories," and if you have not received a visit yet, you will eventually. Do you feel "prepared to make a defense to anyone who calls on you to account for the hope that is in you, yet do it with gentleness and reverence," as Peter exhorts in 1 Peter 3:15 (RSV:CE)? Here's an example of someone who wasn't.

Early on a Saturday morning, a man awakens to the sound of a knock at his door. Not wanting to leave the comfort of his bed, he rolls over and pretends not to hear it. As the knocking grows louder, it becomes evident that his uninvited guests are not planning to leave anytime soon. While still inside, he greets the visitors with a less-than-pleasant "Whaddaya want?" A moment of silence passes. "We need to speak to you about Jehovah" comes the reply. In a minor tantrum, the resident swings open the door, snarls "He's not in!" then shuts the door swiftly and without further comment.

If this approach (or hiding behind the living-room furniture) is what you would consider an appropriate way to deal with a door-to-door proselytizer, then it is time for some improvements.

What hinders people in such situations is often either fear or indifference: indifference, not caring enough to bring their faith to the other; fear, feeling unequipped to provide a convincing defense for the faith. Either way, the difficulty is easily cured. The remedy for indifference is to ask that the Lord give you zeal for souls and love for the faith. Easy enough. Overcoming fear requires more effort. To explain and defend the Catholic faith, you need not enroll in a doctorate program in theology or thoroughly study all the writings of the early Church Fathers. Any number of books and web sites will suffice to give you the confidence to explain your faith to others.[1]

The aim of this book is not so much to provide an exhaustive explanation of Catholic dogma but to familiarize the reader with Watchtower teachings and to equip him with the tools necessary for responding to the average Witness who knocks at the door. To that end, it is helpful to know something about the Jehovah's Witnesses and how their movement started.

Over 350 years had passed since the dawn of the Protestant Reformation, Mormonism had sprouted up decades earlier, and Adventism was seeing its first days. It was the latter part of the 1800s, a century that gave rise to myriad new religious movements. Many of these were concerned with the imminent return of Christ, and virtually all of them felt that the unblemished truth of early Christianity had been encrusted with faulty "traditions of men" (Mark 7:8) and infected with pagan philosophy. The Jehovah's Witnesses saw the Catholic Church as part of "the devil's organization," the Mormons considered it "the grand and abominable church of Satan," while Adventists claimed it was the "whore of Babylon" spoken of in the book of Revelation. Such animosity was commonplace, and it was even predicted by Christ in Matthew: "If they have called the master of the house [Jesus] Beelzebul, how much more will they malign those of his household?" (Matt. 10:25; RSV:CE).

Each of the aforementioned sects (and countless others) felt that God was calling it to rise above all the others to restore his true church, which had allegedly been forced underground for some 1,800 years. In particular, the Witnesses announced that their "beliefs and practices were not new but were a restoration

---

[1] For starters, read *Catholicism and Fundamentalism* by Karl Keating (San Francisco: Ignatius Press, 1988) or *Beginning Apologetics*, vols. 1 and 2, by Fr. Frank Chacon and Jim Burnham (Farmington, New Mexico: San Juan Catholic Seminars, 1993). Also, visit Catholic Answers at *www.catholic.com* or check out the resources at *www.jamesakin.com*.

of first-century Christianity."[2] In 1879, the one who began this lofty task of "restoration" was Charles Taze Russell, the founder of the Jehovah's Witnesses. Under his tutelage, a small band of followers known as Bible Students began spreading doctrines that are now embraced by six million adherents worldwide.

Such teachings include a denial of several core Christian dogmas, including the divinity of Christ, the Trinity, the existence of eternal damnation, the immortal soul, and the hope of all Christians to attain union with God in heaven. What the Witnesses affirm is equally puzzling to those familiar with basic Christianity. For example: Only 144,000 people are going to heaven, and Jesus was Michael the archangel before the Incarnation and is now Michael again.

Despite their odd beliefs, we want to give individual adherents of Watchtower teachings the respect they deserve as human beings. That means being frank with them about the problems with the religious beliefs to which they subscribe. This point is excellently made by the late Catholic apologist Frank Sheed:

> Are a man's religious opinions deserving of respect? The man is, certainly; but his religious opinions may or may not be. The result of a man's thinking on religion is no more necessarily deserving of respect than the result of his thinking in another field. To pretend a respect for it that one does not feel is to treat the man as a child, whose efforts must be taken very seriously lest he burst into tears. In other words, to treat a man's religion with more respect than it deserves is to treat the man with less respect than he deserves.[3]

If you know any Witnesses, you know that they would be the first to endorse the above statement. They have no qualms about denouncing "false religions," and they are quick to defend their doctrines. Ever since the dawn of the Watchtower Bible and Tract

---

[2] *Reasoning from the Scriptures* (Brooklyn: Watchtower Bible and Tract Society of New York, 1985), 203.

[3] Frank Sheed, *Sidelights on the Catholic Revival* (New York: Sheed and Ward, 1940), 84.

Society in the late 1800s, they have been encouraged to pursue truth and place other belief systems under scrutiny:

> It is not a form of religious persecution for anyone to *say* and to *show* that another religion is false. It is not religious persecution for an informed person to expose publicly a certain religion as being false, thus allowing persons to see the difference between false religion and true religion. . . . To make a public exposure of false religion is certainly of more value than exposing a news report as being untrue; it is a public service instead of a religious persecution and it has to do with the eternal life and happiness of the public. Still it leaves the public free to choose.[4]

Although many Witnesses have in practice refused to read or listen to frank examinations of the Watchtower's teachings, the organization has in principle invited such inquiries:

> We have never found fault with any one for specifying what in our teaching was supposed to be error, and for endeavoring earnestly to show wherein we were wrong. All we ask for is fairness and candor.[5]

These are words that should be taken seriously by Witnesses, who have been taught to refuse to consider sources that question their faith. The same is true of the following Watchtower exhortation:

> Error never desires to be investigated. Light always courts a thorough and complete investigation. Light and truth are synonymous.[6]

This may mean that a Witness would need to examine, not only his personal beliefs, but also the teachings of the Watchtower itself:

> We need to examine, not only what we personally believe, but also what is taught by any religious organization with which we may

---

[4] *The Watchtower*, 15 November 1963, 688; italics in original.

[5] *Watchtower Reprints*, 119 (*Zion's Watch Tower*, July 1880, 7).

[6] J. F. Rutherford, *Millions Now Living Will Never Die* (Brooklyn: Watchtower Bible and Tract Society of New York, 1920), 13.

be associated. Are its teachings in full harmony with God's Word, or are they based on the traditions of men? If we are lovers of the truth, there is nothing to fear from such examination. It should be the sincere desire of every one of us to learn what God's will is for us, and then do it.[7]

And if a Witness comes to the conclusion that the Watchtower's teachings are false, that would have implications for his religious affiliation:

> It is obvious that the true God, who is himself "the God of truth" and who hates lies, will not look with favor on persons who cling to organizations that teach falsehood. . . . And, really, would you want to be even associated with a religion that had not been honest with you?[8]

With these quotes and considerations in mind, we are about to embark upon a journey into the world of the Witnesses—their beliefs, their lifestyle, and their history. Most readers of this book will be Christians seeking to answer a friend or relative, but some may be members of the organization who are taking a positive step to explore their doubts about the Watchtower. To them, I offer my prayers, and it is my hope that after all the evidence has been presented, the readers will then have the courage to apply these very same standards in an examination of the Watchtower's teachings.

---

[7] *The Truth That Leads to Eternal Life* (Brooklyn: Watchtower Bible and Tract Society of New York, 1968), 13.

[8] *Is This Life All There Is?* (Brooklyn: Watchtower Bible and Tract Society of New York, 1974), 46.

PART ONE

INSIDE THE WATCHTOWER

Jehovah's Witnesses' Leaders

We begin our study of the Jehovah's Witnesses by looking at the lives and ideas of the six men who have served as presidents of the Watchtower Bible and Tract Society. Much of this is information that Jehovah's Witnesses are not told. However, before beginning our look at the six Watchtower presidents, a disclaimer should be made: Regardless of how righteous or sinful a particular man may be, the level of his personal sanctity does not of itself affect the truth of his beliefs. For example, after Peter professed the identity of Jesus as the Messiah, the Lord gave him the keys of his kingdom—but later called him "Satan" (Matt. 16:15–19, 23). While this episode demonstrated a failure on Peter's part, this failure did not invalidate his belief system or deprive him of his position as Jesus' chief apostle. Just because someone has personal faults, it does not necessarily follow that his theology is bad or that he does not validly hold a particular office in God's organization. In other words, truth is independent of the lifestyle of the one professing it (although the two really should go hand in hand).

Take Satan as another example. Intellectually, he knows more about God than anyone on earth, but obviously his "lifestyle" is wholly evil. His actions, therefore, do not reflect the truth of his theology. On the other hand, an atheist may live a morally upright life but be entirely wrong in his theology (or lack thereof).

This having been said and without presuming to judge hearts, we offer the following information. It is not intended to malign. Though truth and lifestyle are independent, the latter can be relevant when evaluating whether an individual should be trusted as a representative of God. The Lord does not send us representatives, expecting us to believe them, without providing them with credentials. In the Bible, God sometimes sent prophets whom he allowed to work miracles to prove that their messages were from God. He also instituted certain offices, such as high priest and apostle, and authorized the holders of these offices to speak for him. Today, when some leader claims to speak for God, it is pertinent to ask a few questions. Does he hold a divinely instituted office? Has he worked verified miracles? If neither is the case, we are on unsafe ground.

Charles Taze Russell

In 1852, Charles Taze Russell was born in a suburb of Pittsburgh. He reached the seventh grade but then left school permanently to work as a clerk in his father's haberdashery store. Though originally a Presbyterian, Russell converted to Congregationalism, agnosticism, and then Adventism before making a personal discovery that led him to announce that he was the seventh angel of whom John spoke in Revelation, who would usher in the Kingdom of Christ on earth. The other six angels, Russell declared, were the apostles Paul and John, the heretic Arius (condemned by the first Ecumenical Council at Nicaea for denying the divinity of Christ), Peter Waldo (of the gnostic Waldensian sect), John Wycliff, and Martin Luther.

Grand claims were nothing new for Russell. In his earlier days he marketed what he called "miracle wheat" for a dollar a pound (sixty dollars a bushel, which was expensive at that time), promising that it would grow five times faster than regular wheat.[1] The farmers who purchased it soon discovered that it was not miraculous at all, and they sued Russell. In fact, government experts testified that it yielded less than regular wheat.[2] Russell was found guilty and forced to return the money.

---

[1] *The Brooklyn Daily Eagle*, 1 November 1916: obituary.

[2] Ibid., 27 January 1913, 3.

Russell later decided to offer a cure for "surface cancer," saying, "No fee will be charged" for those who wanted the formula, provided that they wrote to him "directly, stating particulars" about their disease. He also marketed alleged cures for typhoid and pneumonia.[3]

Russell married Maria Frances Ackley, but after seventeen years of marriage she sued him for divorce, which the court granted, finding Russell at fault. He appealed this judgment five times, each unsuccessfully.[4] His wife reported that she sought the divorce because of "his conceit, egotism, domination, and improper conduct in relation to other women."[5] The Watchtower's biography of Russell says only that they divorced because "they disagreed about the management of his journal."[6]

Russell's theology and scholarship were also the subject of much scrutiny. A Baptist pastor, J. J. Ross, published a booklet denouncing the "self-styled pastor." In it, Ross claimed that Russell was a pseudo-scholar who "never attended the higher schools of learning; knows comparatively nothing of philosophy, systematic or historical theology, and is totally ignorant of the dead languages."[7] Russell reacted by suing Ross for defamatory libel. According to the records of the High Court of Ontario, in *Russell vs. Ross*, March 17, 1913, the following took place:

During the cross-examination, the defendant's attorney—a gentleman named Staunton—questioned Russell's claim to know Hebrew, Greek, and Latin:

---

[3] *Watchtower Reprints*, 5268 (*The Watch Tower*, 1 July 1913, 199–200); 5689 (*The Watch Tower*, 15 May 1915, 151–52); 5691 (*The Watch Tower*, 15 May 1915, 154–55).

[4] *Dictionary of American Biography* (Oxford: Oxford University Press, 1935), vol. 16.

[5] Bruce M. Metzger, cited in Anthony Hoeckema, *The Four Major Cults* (Grand Rapids: Eerdmans, 1963), 227.

[6] Charles Taze Russell, *Studies in the Scriptures* (Brooklyn: Watchtower Bible and Tract Society of New York, 1925–1927), 1:1–30.

[7] J. J. Ross, *Some Facts about the Self-Styled 'Pastor' Charles Taze Russell* (Hamilton, Ontario: self-published, 1912), 3–4.

STAUNTON: "Do you know the Greek Alphabet?"
RUSSELL: "Oh Yes."
STAUNTON: "Can you tell me the correct letters if you see them?"
RUSSELL: "Some of them, I might make a mistake on some of them."
STAUNTON: "Would you tell me the names of those on top of the page, page 447, that I have got here?"
RUSSELL: "Well, I don't know that I would be able to."
STAUNTON: "You can't tell what those letters are, look at them and see if you know?"
RUSSELL: "My way . . ." [interrupted]
STAUNTON: "Are you familiar with the Greek language?"
RUSSELL: "No."

Pressing Russell still further, Staunton brought him to admit that "he knew nothing about Latin and Hebrew, and that he had never taken a course in philosophy or systematic theology much less attended schools of higher learning."[8] Though Russell considered it a libelous charge to say that he never attended schools of higher learning, he admitted under examination that he left school at the age of fourteen and that he had had only seven years of education.

The cross-examination continued:

STAUNTON: "Is it true that you were never ordained?"
RUSSELL: "It is not true."

However, Russell's answer changed when the question was put to him more specifically.

STAUNTON: "Now, you never were ordained by a bishop, clergyman, presbytery, council, or any body of men living?"
RUSSELL: "I never was."

In the same manner, Staunton further questioned Russell on the topic of his divorce and alimony. Russell first swore that his wife did not divorce him and that the court did not grant her alimony

---

[8] Walter Martin, *The Kingdom of the Cults* (Minneapolis: Bethany Fellowship, 1970), 39.

from him. Upon further cross-examination, he admitted the opposite. Russell originally claimed that all the charges against him were false, yet he was forced to admit the truth of them before the court.

Disturbed by the idea of hell, Russell departed from orthodox Christianity and began learning the teachings of a man named Jonas Wendell. Wendell was associated with the Second Adventists, a group of denominations stemming from the teachings of William Miller, who predicted the return of Christ in 1843 and 1844. In his magazine, Russell mentioned Wendell's preaching:

> Seemingly by accident, one evening I dropped into a dusty, dingy hall, where I had heard religious services were held, to see if the handful who met there had anything more sensible to offer than the creeds of the great churches. There, for the first time, I heard something of the views of Second Adventists, the preacher being Mr. Jonas Wendell.[9]

The nineteenth century was replete with religious movements predicting the end of the world. After Miller's failed predictions for the years 1843 and 1844, other Adventists were looking to 1874 as the date of Christ's Second Coming (also known as the Parousia). It, too, came and went. But this date took on a greater significance for Russell after an Adventist named Nelson Barbour convinced him that Jesus did return in 1874—*invisibly*: "Russell's study group had come to realize that when Christ returned it would not be in the flesh, as commonly believed. . . . [W]hen Jesus should come he would be as invisible as though an angel had come."[10]

The Adventist magazine *Herald of the Morning* (published by Barbour) taught that Christ returned in October of 1874. Russell accepted this, as well as the theory that all believers would be raptured ("caught up" bodily to be with Christ in the heavens) in the spring of 1878. After this failed to happen, Barbour

---

[9] *Watchtower Reprints*, 3821 (*Zion's Watch Tower*, 15 July 1906, 229–30).

[10] *Jehovah's Witnesses in the Divine Purpose* (Brooklyn: Watchtower Bible and Tract Society of New York, 1959), 18.

and Russell separated in 1879, and Russell started the magazine *Zion's Watch Tower and Herald of Christ's Presence*.[11] The mention of Christ's presence in the title stressed the teaching, now rejected by Jehovah's Witnesses, that Jesus had been invisibly present on earth since 1874.

Russell quickly cast off his Adventist association, and his followers came to be known as Bible Students, claiming the full title "International Bible Students Association." He began writing voluminously, producing several books, including the *Millennial Dawn Series*, later renamed *Studies in the Scriptures*. Russell penned six of the seven volumes in this series,[12] which is replete with bizarre teachings now rejected by the Watchtower. Yet at the time, the Watchtower reported this about Russell: "He said that he could never have written his books himself. It all came from God, through the enlightenment of the Holy Spirit."[13]

In one of these volumes, Russell explains how the Great Pyramid of Giza can be used to predict end-times events by calculating the length of its various internal passageways.[14] It was to be considered "God's Stone Witness and Prophet, the Great Pyramid in Egypt [from Is. 19:19, 20]."[15] *The Watch Tower* also confirmed this view: "Indeed, some, after reading this volume [*Studies in the Scriptures*, vol. 3], have referred to the Great Pyramid as 'The Bible in stone.' "[16] It also noted:

---

[11] The Watchtower later decided that Nelson Barbour was "the evil servant" of Matt. 24:48–51. See *Studies in the Scriptures* (*The Finished Mystery*), (Brooklyn: People's Pulpit Association, 1917), 7:386.

[12] The seventh volume was published after Russell's death. When Russell died, his followers splintered into a number of groups. Some of them maintain that volume seven is his work and is therefore authoritative, while others claim it was authored by another and is therefore not authoritative. It is likely that Russell did not write this seventh volume.

[13] *Studies in the Scriptures* (*The Finished Mystery*), 7:387.

[14] Charles Taze Russell, *Studies in the Scriptures* (Brooklyn: Watchtower Bible and Tract Society, 1891), 3:362–64.

[15] Ibid., 313.

[16] *Watchtower Reprints*, 4790 (*The Watch Tower*, 15 March 1911, 95).

Viewed from whatever standpoint we please, the Great Pyramid is certainly the most remarkable building in the world. . . . [I]t acquires new interest to every Christian advanced in the study of God's word. . . . The Great Pyramid, however, proves to be a store-house of important truth—scientific, historic, and prophetic—and its testimony is found to be in perfect accord with the Bible. . . . [I]t is a strong *corroborative witness* to God's plan; and few students can carefully examine it, marking the harmony of its testimony with that of the written Word, without feeling impressed that its con-struction was planned and directed by the same divine wisdom. . . . [I]t was evidently a part of God's purpose to keep secret, until the Time of the End.[17]

While Russell taught that God placed the pyramid in Egypt,[18] shortly after he died the Watchtower made a drastic change and declared that the pyramid was built under the direction of Satan.[19] Those who modeled their beliefs on the pyramid's structure were "not following after Christ," since it was "Satan's Bible."[20] How-ever, if the Watchtower's assertion about being "God's organiza-tion" is true, one is left with the stark contradiction that God's organization was using "Satan's Bible" and "not following after Christ" during those years when it taught the pyramid was, in fact, God's stone witness.

Russell's *Studies in the Scriptures* are not often found in Kingdom Hall libraries today, and if they are present, not much attention is paid to them. This fact is uncharacteristic of the Watchtower's earlier history, as it used to speak very highly of them. For exam-ple, in 1910 *The Watch Tower* noted:

[T]hey are not merely comments on the Bible, but they are prac-tically the Bible itself. . . . Furthermore, not only do we find that people cannot see the divine plan in studying the Bible by itself, but we see, also, that if anyone lays the SCRIPTURE STUDIES aside, even

---

[17] *Studies in the Scriptures (Thy Kingdom Come)*, (Brooklyn: Watchtower Bible and Tract Society of New York, 1891) 3:314–15.

[18] *Watchtower Reprints*, 525 (*Zion's Watch Tower*, September 1883, 3).

[19] *The Watch Tower*, 15 November 1928, 339–45.

[20] Ibid., 341, 344.

after he has used them, after he has become familiar with them, after he has read them for ten years—if he then lays them aside and ignores them and goes to the Bible alone, though he has understood his Bible for ten years, our experience shows that within two years he goes into darkness. On the other hand, if he had merely read the SCRIPTURE STUDIES with their references, and has not read a page of the Bible, as such, he will be in the light at the end of two years, because he would have the light of the Scriptures.[21]

Though the Watchtower had considered Charles Taze Russell to be the faithful servant our Lord spoke of in Matthew 24:45–47,[22] much of Russell's teaching is now considered erroneous. For that reason, the Watchtower seeks to avoid any mention of Russell or his teachings. Its publication *Awake!* magazine asks, "Who is preaching the teaching of Pastor Russell? Certainly not Jehovah's Witnesses! They cannot be accused of following him, for they neither quote him as an authority nor publish nor distribute his writings."[23]

Russell passed away on a train on October 31, 1916, while wearing a toga made from bedsheets. In an issue of *The Watch Tower* published immediately after his death, one of his followers stated that "like the disciples of old our own hearts burned within us as we listened to his clear and beautiful unfolding of the Word of God. We thus learned that we were sitting at the feet of God, and also the greatest Bible scholar since the days of the apostles."[24] Though this esteem has largely dissipated and much of his theology has been left behind, his gravesite in a suburb of Pittsburgh is impressive. A stone pyramid weighing several tons stands beside the tomb.

---

[21] *Watchtower Reprints*, 4685 (*The Watch Tower*, 15 September 1910, 298).

[22] See *Watchtower Reprints*, 1 November 1917, 6159; also see the 1911 *Convention Report of the Jehovah's Witnesses*.

[23] *Awake!*, 8 May 1951, 26.

[24] *Watchtower Reprints*, 6009 (*The Watch Tower*, 1 December 1916, 370).

"Judge" Joseph Rutherford

Following the death of Russell, and despite a great deal of opposition from various members of the Watchtower, Joseph Franklin Rutherford succeeded him in 1917. "Judge" Rutherford (formerly the legal advisor of the organization) was a Missouri attorney who was raised Baptist. He began his judicial career as a court stenographer. On the basis of this experience he applied to be admitted as a member of the Missouri Bar, which he was, on May 5, 1892.[25] It should be noted that Rutherford did not attend law school or receive any law degree, but—as was the practice in his day—he merely sat in as an "acting" circuit court judge for four days during the regular judge's absence: "In other words, he was permitted to sit in the place of the Judge. He did not preside over the Circuit Court in his own name or in his own right."[26]

Once Rutherford was at the helm, he replaced the former elders with his own appointees and unseated the majority of the Watchtower directors. A few splinter groups formed at this time, claiming to hold fast to Russell's theology. To distinguish his group from the offshoots, he gave the International Bible Students a new name while at a convention in Columbus, Ohio, on Saturday, July 26, 1931. From then on, they were to be known as "Jehovah's witnesses" [sic]. (Jehovah's Witnesses have also been known as Millennial Dawnists, Russellites, Dawnites, Watchtower People, and Standfasters. Approximately a dozen groups have split off since the time of Russell, including the Laymen's Home Missionary Movement, Associated Bible Students, and the Dawn Bible Students Association.)

Rutherford is most often remembered for his slogan and book *Millions Now Living Will Never Die*. These promoted his "posi-

---

[25] Rev. Edward Lodge Curran, *Judge "for Four Days" Rutherford* (reprint, Clayton, California: Witness, Inc., n.d.), 4–5.

[26] Ibid., 5.

tive and indisputable conclusion"[27] that millions of people alive in 1914 would live to see Armageddon (the final battle between God and Satan) and paradise restored. All Witnesses held this doctrine until the mid-1990s, when the last members of that generation died off.

Rutherford was also known for promoting evangelism by record player. Jehovah's Witnesses would stand with a record player at the doorstep of a person's house and play a segment of one of Rutherford's recordings for the potential convert. Rutherford thought it was important that others hear him, since he taught that he was the mouthpiece of Jehovah for this age, God having designated Rutherford's words as the expression of the divine mandate.[28]

The Watchtower has made many predictions that never saw fulfillment, and one of its most blatant errors was Rutherford's prediction that Abraham, Isaac, and Jacob would return to earth in 1925. Since the patriarchs were allegedly coming, he figured they would need transportation and a place to stay. He therefore bought them a car and built a mansion for them in San Diego, California, calling it *Beth Sarim* ("House of the Princes").[29] When the patriarchs failed to show up to claim the house, Rutherford decided to live there during the Great Depression.

In a 1984 issue of *The Watchtower*, a Witness named Karl Klein spoke of his memories of Rutherford and commented that, "regarding his misguided statements as to what we could expect in 1925, he once confessed to us at Bethel, 'I made an ass of myself.' "[30]

---

[27] J. F. Rutherford, *Millions Now Living Will Never Die* (Brooklyn: Watchtower Bible and Tract Society of New York, 1920), 97.

[28] Rutherford, *Why Serve Jehovah?* (Brooklyn: Watchtower Bible and Tract Society of New York, 1932), 62.

[29] Rutherford, *Salvation* (Brooklyn: Watchtower Bible and Tract Society of New York, 1939), 311.

[30] 1 October 1984, 24 (footnote).

Nathan Knorr

During Rutherford's presidency, much of Russell's theology fell by the wayside. The same happened with Rutherford's theology when Nathan Homer Knorr was elected president after Rutherford's death in 1942. Under Knorr's leadership, the Witnesses grew from 115,000 to 2.5 million, largely due to the change in methods of evangelization. He dropped the record-playing technique and developed training programs for the members, equipping them to deliver persuasive speeches at the doorstep. Under Knorr, Watchtower vice-president Frederick Franz bumped the date of Christ's return from 1874 to 1914, and the year 1975 began to be seen by many as the date of Armageddon and the end of the world. From 1950 to 1961, Knorr led a group of three others to compose the *New World Translation* (NWT), a translation of the Bible used only by the Watchtower.

Frederick Franz

Franz was the first Watchtower president to have attended college (two years), and he was also on the committee of "translators" that produced the NWT. He began his presidency shortly after the disgruntled membership saw another prophetic date, 1975, come and go without fulfillment. At this time, many—even within the Brooklyn headquarters—began to question the organization's chronology and its various prophetic dates. The Watchtower began losing hundreds of thousands of members, seeing the first-ever decline in membership.

So, the Governing Body (the leaders of the Watchtower) and Franz began to strategize. They broke up the Bible studies of several important and high-ranking Jehovah's Witnesses who had grown increasingly doubtful of the Watchtower's teachings. These "dissenters" were then put before formal Watchtower Judicial Committees to face charges of "apostasy." The committees disfellowshipped Raymond Franz (Governing Body member and nephew of President Frederick Franz). Another was invited to leave, and a prominent writer for the Society was cast out as well. Shortly after this incident, the Watchtower decided to keep the rank-and-file membership in check by distributing over ten million copies of *The Watchtower* magazine, which contained stern reminders to the Witnesses, warning them all to "avoid independent thinking" and observing that those who fail to follow the counsel of "God's visible organization" (i.e., the Watchtower) are guilty of a rebellious attitude stemming from Satan.[31]

Milton Henschel

When Franz passed away in 1992, he was succeeded by Milton Henschel, who was 72 years old when elected. One of the more notable occurrences during Henschel's presidency was that the Watchtower dropped its teaching about the generation of 1914— that those people alive in 1914 (allegedly the date of Christ's invisible return) would live to see Armageddon take place. In 2000, Milton Henschel stepped down from his position of president of the Watchtower Bible and Tract Society of Pennsylvania and was replaced by longtime Witness Don Adams. Henschel remains a member of the Governing Body, which now consists of thirteen men.

When the organization began in the nineteenth century, the president filled the role of a spiritual and administrative leader. As it grew, presidents sought more advisors, and eventually the Governing Body was formed. Now the Governing Body focuses more on the spiritual and doctrinal leadership of the Witnesses, whereas the president is more involved in the business and legal aspects the organization. When the movement spread to other countries, new "corporations" were established, each with its own president. Now there are several corporations in the U.S. alone, and Don

---

[31] *The Watchtower*, 1 January 1983, 22.

Adams is president of the largest one, the Watchtower Bible and Tract Society of Pennsylvania.

Today, the average age of Governing Body members is about eighty. Thus, the Watchtower will soon see a decisive change in leadership. Decades ago Joseph Rutherford declared that the "heavenly calling" of the 144,000 ended in 1935,[32] so anyone baptized after that date is not part of the anointed class, from which leaders were to be selected. It was once held that only people who were born before the 1920s were supposed to be Watchtower leaders. As of 1998, there were 8,756 people who claimed to be part of the 144,000, and from this pool of aging Witnesses the Governing Body has chosen its members. How the Watchtower will choose to deal with the problem created by the dwindling pool of those in the anointed class remains to be seen.

---

[32] Under Rutherford, a two-class system developed, consisting of (1) the "anointed class," who comprise what the Watchtower sees as a literal 144,000-member group (based on Rev. 7 and 14), which will rule with Christ in the heavens (i.e., a heavenly hope or calling); and (2) the "other sheep," or "great crowd," which consists of countless millions who will reside forever on a paradise earth (i.e., an earthly hope).

2

Inside the Organization

The Kingdom Hall

Jehovah's Witnesses meet for five hours each week in what are called Kingdom Halls, not churches.[1] These are large meeting rooms devoid of any religious art or stained glass. Upon entering, the stranger is met with many smiles and greetings from well-dressed Witnesses who cordially refer to each other as "brother" and "sister." Suit and tie are standard attire for gentlemen at the Sunday morning gathering, which begins with a brief prayer and then a song. Any of the 225 songs written by the Watchtower will be sung, including "Loyally Submitting to Theocratic Order" (No. 8 in the Witnesses' songbook), "We Are Jehovah's Witnesses" (No. 113), or "Theocracy's Increase" (No. 53).

Following the song, the elder of a local congregation gives a 45-minute lecture, followed by a short break. The meeting resumes with a review of an article from the most recent issue of *The Watchtower* magazine. An elder and his assistant read the article aloud, paragraph by paragraph, and the congregation is invited to help answer the questions posed at the bottom of the pages. (These questions are taken almost verbatim from the text and therefore can easily be answered by anyone who has been following along.) A microphone is passed around the hall to members who raise their hands to volunteer answers. By using this approach, the Watchtower seeks to build "spiritual maturity" among its mem-

---

[1] Witnesses also prefer to be identified as God's "organization," not as a church or denomination. These name changes are examples of the efforts the Watchtower makes to separate itself from "apostate Christendom."

bers, since they gain a sense of confidence in their understanding Watchtower teachings. No collection is taken up—Witnesses often point this out to visitors. The entire Sunday morning meeting takes two hours. Following it, Witnesses often pair up and head into the neighborhoods with hefty stacks of *Watchtower* and *Awake!* magazines to be distributed, or "placed."

The format of the Sunday meetings reveals that the Watchtower's primary intention is to use that time to teach the members. Of the two hours, less than five minutes are spent in prayer. The remaining hour and fifty-five minutes are for learning Watchtower doctrine. Though the Kingdom Hall is said to be a place of *worship*, very little actually takes place there. Though the individual members may be prayerful people, after two hours on a Sunday morning have been spent on lectures and magazine studies, one may still feel he has not yet "been to church." In fact, ex-Witnesses often comment that this dryness left them longing for a deeper and more sacral form of worship.

Book Study

The next commitment in the weekly schedule of a Witness is a "neighborhood book study" on either a Monday or a Tuesday evening. If a person has accepted a magazine at the door from a Witness and spoken with him a few times, this will most likely be the first meeting at the Kingdom Hall to which the prospective convert is invited. During this one-hour period, a member of the congregation called a "book study overseer" leads the others in a study of two or three chapters from a Watchtower publication, such as *The Greatest Man Who Ever Lived*. This book moves chronologically through the life of Jesus, giving scriptural citations and quotes in the midst of the commentary provided by the Watchtower. After each chapter is read, the same question-and-answer format that was used on Sunday follows, and a portion of the Bible is read *in conjunction with* the Watchtower's interpretation of it.

For example, *The Greatest Man Who Ever Lived* points out that

Jesus told his followers, "Have no fear, little flock, because your Father has approved of giving you the kingdom" (Luke 12:32). The next sentence continues, "He thus reveals that only a relatively small number (later identified as 144,000) will be in the heavenly Kingdom. The majority of the ones who receive eternal life will be earthly subjects of the Kingdom." The first question at the end of the chapter asks, "How many make up the 'little flock' and what do they receive?"[2] Thus, the study of Luke 12 concludes with the members of the congregation saying that only 144,000 people go to heaven, while the remainder stay on earth (though Luke 12 says nothing of the matter).

The book study is essentially another study of Watchtower doctrine intermingled with biblical verses that are regularly taken out of context. Unfortunately, Witnesses usually do not have a background in biblical studies prior to joining the organization. As a result, they are less likely to notice when the Watchtower reads too much into a biblical text.

Theocratic Ministry School and Service Meeting

On either Wednesday or Thursday, the Witnesses again meet at the Kingdom Hall for the final session of the week. During this two-hour meeting, they practice delivering speeches and are evaluated by one another in front of the congregation. Role-playing exercises are performed to prepare the Witnesses for situations they may encounter while evangelizing. Following the talks and skits, members may exchange evangelization tips and share experiences from the past week of field service.

Home Bible Studies

Beyond the five hours per week spent in meetings, Witnesses are strongly encouraged to be out "in the field," passing out mag-

---

[2] *The Greatest Man Who Ever Lived* (Brooklyn: Watchtower Bible and Tract Society of New York, 1991), chap. 78.

azines and setting up home Bible studies with prospective converts. All Witnesses who spend time evangelizing are required to keep records of how much time they have spent going door-to-door, how many times "back-calls" have been made to prospective converts' houses; how many magazines have been "placed," etc. These records are submitted to the local Kingdom Hall and eventually forwarded to the headquarters in Brooklyn.

The private meetings conducted in people's homes are called "Bible studies," but in actuality they are a forum where yet another Watchtower publication is studied and some Bible verses are offered in support of what the particular publication says.

A book such as *Knowledge That Leads to Everlasting Life*[3] is read, and the question-and-answer format is again employed after the reading of each chapter. A member of the congregation directs the lesson, which was composed by the Watchtower in Brooklyn. The structured subject matter and specific questions at the bottom of each page ensure that there will be minimal deviation or opportunity for disagreement and open discussion. The answers expected are to consist of a member's explaining in his own words a point made in the book. In practice, this discussion is not a matter of sharing personal exegesis but of repeating Watchtower teaching back to the official. The questions are simple enough that even those who have never read a page of the Bible will quickly feel they are beginning to master Scripture.

Disfellowshipping

If a member of the congregation is suspected of a grievous fault (such as deviating from Watchtower teaching, going to a Christian church service, entering the military, committing adultery, saluting the flag, reading books from ex-Witnesses, eating with suspected dissenters, or—until recently—receiving a blood transfusion), he is to be brought to the Kingdom Hall to be questioned

---

[3] *Knowledge That Leads to Everlasting Life* (Brooklyn: Watchtower Bible and Tract Society of New York, 1995).

by a group of leading members of the congregation, known as the Judicial Committee. If found guilty, he is disfellowshipped (excommunicated). In 1986, for example, the organization reported that 36,638 individuals had been disfellowshipped the previous year, "the greater number of them for practicing immorality."[4]

The Watchtower's position on the treatment of disfellowshipped members has varied over time. In 1920, the Watchtower said, "We would not refuse to treat one as a brother because he did not believe the Society is the Lord's channel. . . . If others see it in a different way, that is their privilege. There should be full liberty of conscience."[5] By 1930, one who disagreed with the Watchtower was to be classed as an "evil servant" and placed alongside the "son of perdition" whose fate is "destruction."[6]

Currently, Witnesses are to consider a disfellowshipped person, effectively, as if dead. While he may attend the weekly meetings, others are forbidden to speak with him in the Kingdom Hall: "Those who are acquainted with the situation in the congregation should never say 'Hello' or 'Good-by' to him. He is not welcome in our midst, we avoid him."[7] This shunning includes family members (both immediate and extended), friends, and business acquaintances. Over time, and after having expressed repentance, the disfellowshipped person may be restored to the congregation when the Judicial Committee sees fit.

Ex-Witnesses point out that while disfellowshipping may sound good on paper (it is supposedly based on various biblical injunctions to separate an unrepentant sinner from the faith community), in practice it is applied in an overly rigid manner, resulting in a cruel form of discipline that has caused the breakup of families and fails to respect the dignity of the disfellowshipped person.

---

[4] *The Watchtower*, 1 January 1986, 13.

[5] *The Watch Tower*, 1 April 1920, 100–101.

[6] Ibid., 15 September 1930, 275–81.

[7] *The Watchtower*, 1 March 1952, 141. See also "If a Relative Is Disfellowshipped," 15 September 1981, 26–31.

Hierarchy

Local congregations of Jehovah's Witnesses include up to two hundred members. Once there are more than two hundred, a new congregation is usually formed. "Spiritually mature men" serve as elders of each congregation, which they supervise. About twenty congregations together form what is called a circuit, and about ten circuits form a district. These are all, in turn, ruled by the Governing Body, which is made up of longtime Witnesses. The headquarters of the Watchtower Bible and Tract Society, known as "Bethel" (Hebrew for "house of God"), is located in Brooklyn, New York.

To understand the nature of the Jehovah's Witnesses' hierarchy, one must realize the significance of the Watchtower organization in the minds of its adherents. The heart of its doctrinal system is the belief that Jehovah God has categorically, emphatically, and unequivocally used the Watchtower as his "mouthpiece" to the nations, as his "prophet," and as his sole "channel of communication." The Watchtower organization, under the direction of the Governing Body, is understood to be the "faithful and discreet slave" spoken of in Matthew 24:45. This slave, it is believed, has been commissioned by Jehovah God to provide "spiritual food" continually by means of Watchtower publications to the millions of followers, who are known as "domestics."

The Watchtower teaches that it serves as "God's visible organization." All adherents are led to believe that God "does not impart his holy spirit and understanding and appreciation of his Word apart from his visible organization."[8] The organization has made many other strong claims for itself throughout the years, such as the following:

> Consider, too, the fact that Jehovah's organization alone, in all the earth, is directed by God's holy spirit or active force. Only this organization functions for Jehovah's purposes and to his praise.[9]

---

[8] Ibid., 1 July 1965, 391.
[9] Ibid., 1 July 1973, 402.

> All who want to understand the Bible should appreciate that the "greatly diversified wisdom of God" can be known only through Jehovah's channel of communication, the faithful and discreet slave.[10]

> Theocratic ones will appreciate the Lord's visible organization and not be so foolish as to pit against Jehovah's channel their own human reasoning and sentiment and personal feelings.[11]

> However, not everyone will be permitted to live in the Paradise earth. Requirements must be met. . . . A third requirement is that we *be associated with God's channel*, his organization. . . . To receive everlasting life in the earthly Paradise we must identify that organization and serve God as part of it.[12]

Through the weekly reading of Watchtower teachings, the Witness is led to believe that his salvation is wholly contingent upon his association with the Watchtower. If he rejects it, he rejects Jehovah. If he does not serve it, he is not serving God. For this reason, it is often psychologically difficult for a Witness to leave the organization. Even when a member does learn the truth about the Watchtower, he still finds it hard to leave the organization, in part because he has been so strongly indoctrinated to believe that there is nowhere else to go for spiritual "food."

Publications

Anyone who has spent much time walking through downtown city streets has likely come across Witnesses passing out copies of *Awake!* and *The Watchtower*. These two magazines, the main publications of the Witnesses, are issued on a staggered bi-weekly basis. In 1879, the first copy of the *Watch Tower* consisted of a printing run of 6,000 copies per month. Now printed in 132 languages, 22 million copies of each edition of *The Watchtower* are published monthly. It is primarily doctrinal in nature, and its columns constantly contain articles that attempt to show how the teachings

---

[10] Ibid., 1 October 1994, 8.

[11] Ibid., 1 February 1952, 80.

[12] Ibid., 15 February 1983, 12.

of the churches of Christendom are not in line with the Bible. *Awake!* is more of a general-interest magazine and tends to be less doctrinal in content. It was first known as *The Golden Age* before its name was changed to *Consolation* in 1937 and then to *Awake!* in 1946. Though the magazines used to be sold to prospective converts, they have been given out free of charge since 1990, but Witnesses do ask for donations for them. These donations are then forwarded to the Watchtower, even though the Witnesses themselves typically make a contribution for the literature when they pick it up at their Kingdom Hall—meaning that the Watchtower may be paid twice for the same piece of material.

Since the presses are run exclusively by volunteers, the Watchtower is able to produce a high volume of publications quite inexpensively. Some ex-Witnesses who have had experience with these presses and know how much they cost to run have reported that the Watchtower, through donations received for its publications, makes up for the production costs several times over. In other words, the Watchtower is not being honest when it tells its members that donations received for its literature fall short of the cost of production.[13]

The Watchtower Bible and Tract Society is the largest private publisher ever, having printed over one billion pieces of literature since 1920. Regarding the content of these publications, the Watchtower's approach leaves much to be desired. First, virtually all material is written anonymously, which leaves the reader unable to verify an author's credentials or reputation. In other words, the reader has no way to ascertain if a given author is qualified to write on the subject matter at hand. (Bear in mind that these publications represent *official* Watchtower teaching and doctrine.)

Second, these authors are notorious for quoting scholars out

---

[13] See, for example, see Randall Watters' articles "The Watchtower Way of Laundering Money," at *www.freeminds.org/history/launder.htm*, and "How the Watchtower Was Financed (pre-1990)," at *www.freeminds.org/history/money.htm*. These articles respectively appeared in the June-August 1995 issue of *Free Minds Journal* (with additional notes made December 8, 1996) and in the July/August 1986 *Bethel Ministries Newsletter*.

of context and for quoting as authorities obscure individuals who lack scholarly credentials. Since the average Witness has no formal background in theology and generally does not read non-Watchtower material, he trusts that the literature originating from the Brooklyn headquarters is top-notch scholarship and accurate in what it cites from other sources. This trust is not well founded.

One example of a significant Watchtower blunder in this regard involves the case of Johannes Greber, a spiritist. With the help of his wife, a spirit medium, Greber published a translation of the New Testament. For decades, the Watchtower appealed to Greber's rendering of John 1:1 to support its own reading of the same verse in the NWT. Both versions rendered the last part of this verse as "the Word was *a* god" (emphasis added) rather than "the Word was God," thus making Jesus a mere creature. The Watchtower later recommended that Greber not be cited any longer because he arrived at his translations through communication with messengers from the spirit world.[14] Though the Watchtower knew of Greber's background in 1955,[15] it continued to cite him for support[16] up to 1983.

Peculiar Doctrines and Practices

When a pair of Witnesses come to the door of a prospective convert, it may take some time before the missionaries disclose that they are Jehovah's Witnesses. This is understandably a wise tactic, considering the stigma that has been associated with their organization. Their connection with the Watchtower, however, is not the only thing they hesitate to reveal. A litany of peculiar

---

[14] *The Watchtower*, 1 April 1983, 31.

[15] Ibid., 1 October 1955, 603. See also 15 February 1956, 110–11.

[16] See NWT, 1961 ed.; "'The Word': Who Is He? According to John" (Brooklyn: Watchtower Bible and Tract Society of New York, 1962), 5; *Aid to Bible Understanding* (Brooklyn: Watchtower Bible and Tract Society of New York, 1971), 1134, 1669; and *The Watchtower*, 15 September 1962, 554; 15 October 1975, 640; and 15 April 1976, 231.

doctrines and practices is also not mentioned until things have progressed favorably for some time.

Among the teachings not initially discussed are these: Jesus is really Michael the archangel; the doctrine of the Trinity is pagan in origin; the Holy Spirit is not a person but only God's active force; there is no hell; all the unsaved are simply annihilated. They further claim that man has no immortal soul and that, while many will live in paradise on earth, you will go to heaven only if you are one of the 144,000 anointed ones.[17]

Witnesses assert that Jesus' Second Coming happened when World War I began (1914) but that his return was invisible. Witnesses may not vote, salute the flag, accept a blood transfusion, or celebrate any holiday or birthday, since they hold that these practices displease God. The Watchtower asserts that the source of Christmas music is Satan himself. Witnesses run no children's hospitals, orphanages, food banks, homes for the dying, etc., as to do so is seen as polishing the brass on a sinking ship (since Armageddon is right around the corner). It is better to preach about the coming of the kingdom, where there will be no pain or sorrow.

With such an outlook on the poor, one can only think of our Lord's words in Matthew's Gospel:

> For I became hungry, but YOU[18] gave me nothing to eat, and I got thirsty, and YOU gave me nothing to drink. I was a stranger, but YOU did not receive me hospitably; naked, but YOU did not clothe me; sick and in prison, but YOU did not look after me. . . . Truly I say to YOU, To the extent that YOU did not do it to one of these least ones, YOU did not do it to me. (Matt. 25:42–43, 45)

---

[17] Those who end up on earth (the resurrected ones and those who survive Armageddon) will be allowed to live in paradise for only a thousand years. Then God releases Satan and his minions, giving the people another test. If they pass this, they live forever. See *The Truth That Leads to Eternal Life* (Brooklyn: Watchtower Bible and Tract Society of New York, 1968), 112–13.

[18] The Witnesses' *New World Translation* indicates second person plural by setting YOU and YOUR in small capitals.

James adds:

> If a brother or sister is in a naked state and lacking the food sufficient for the day, yet a certain one of YOU says to them: "Go in peace, keep warm and well fed," but YOU do not give them the necessities for [their] body, of what benefit is it? Thus, too, faith, if it does not have works, is dead in itself. (Jas. 2:15–17)

Technique

The Watchtower strongly encourages the members of the congregation to be out placing magazines and building up the kingdom: "While fellow witnesses of Jehovah are engaging in theocratic pursuits, are you and your family often heading for some recreation spot?"[19] The Witnesses, who often travel in pairs, are instructed to give out magazines to potential converts and then ask questions in hopes of finding common ground. Initial contact is made by asking about the present condition of the world and the prospects for improvement.

In an effort to make their presentation seem relevant to the hearer's life, these questions often target concerns that virtually every person thinks about at some time. For example, Witnesses may ask, "Wouldn't life be different without child abuse, suffering, sickness, war, etc.?" or "How would you like to live in paradise forever?" or "Do you think men will ever live together in peace on earth?" If the person takes literature or seems interested, the fact is recorded on a "House to House Record" form, and they return with a "back-call" in about a week's time. Then they begin to study the Bible with the prospective convert—using Watchtower books. The recruit is now on his way to being "a sheep," someone receptive to their teaching, in contrast to "a goat," who is unreceptive (cf. Matt. 25:31–46, RSV:CE).

If all goes well, the person is invited to the Kingdom Hall meetings and will eventually be baptized by full immersion. At times the baptisms are done "in the name of the Father, and of

---

[19] *The Watchtower*, 1 June 1985, 12.

the Son, and of the Spirit-directed organization," but this formula is not used universally. In some cases, no formula is used, but two questions are asked. The first concerns repentance of sin and willingness to do God's will. The second question is, "Do you understand that your dedication and baptism identify you as one of Jehovah's Witnesses in association with God's Spirit-directed organization?" Upon answering in the affirmative, the inductee is submerged.

In both their literature and conversations, Witnesses often spend more time pointing out the shortcomings of various Christian churches and tearing down the "apostate doctrines of Christendom" than building a case for the Watchtower's theology. If the destructive comments are removed, remarkably little is presented that actually constructs the Watchtower's case. Since there is so little supporting evidence for their theology, it is necessary for Witnesses to attack the opposition instead. To equip their followers for such a task, they use the book *Reasoning from the Scriptures* (a revised version of the earlier publication *Make Sure of All Things*). It provides direction for the members on how to lead a conversation, answer common objections, explain failed predictions, change the subject, interpret the Bible, etc. Witnesses who knock at your door have this book in their briefcases. It is arranged topically. Between three and five Scripture verses are referenced in their Bibles to support each of the Watchtower's main teachings.

Since all the work has been done for them in this publication, the Witnesses can spend their time committing this material to memory. The sheer number of times they use these references in their door-to-door work makes them adept at wielding these passages, giving the impression that they are well versed in Scripture. But the reality is that the average Witness has simply memorized stock answers and approaches to common questions and comments that surface at a prospective convert's doorstep. Outside of these memorized passages, most Witnesses have sparse knowledge of what the whole of Scripture says on the same topics. Unfortunately, as the average person today tends to be biblically illiterate, people capable of using a few memorized verses are seen as virtual Bible scholars.

Statistics

In 1874, there were a total of thirty members joined to the cause of Charles Taze Russell. As of 1998, the Watchtower claimed 5,888,650 "publishers"[20] and fourteen million "adherents." The difference between a publisher and an adherent is that the publishers are active members, while the number of adherents includes not only the publishers but also those who do little more than attend the annual Memorial Service of the Lord—the Witnesses' equivalent of a Holy Thursday celebration. All members and prospective converts are expected to attend this annual service (usually held in March), but only members of the anointed class may partake of the bread and wine. As of 1999, there were 8,756 self-proclaimed members of the anointed class who partook of the bread and wine at the memorial. According to the Watchtower, these "anointed" are the only living people who have the hope of going to heaven.

According to the *1999 Yearbook of Jehovah's Witnesses*, the average Witness spent 204 hours preaching (evangelizing) in 1998. Seven hundred thousand "pioneers" added additional hours to this figure, having spent an average of seventy hours per month in the field. This is a grand total of one billion hours of evangelization done by less than six million people in one year. Included in this statistic are more than four million Bible studies that were conducted by Witnesses.

Despite these efforts, only one of every eighteen Witnesses led a convert to baptism in 1998, including the baptisms of family members. This means that an average 3,796 hours were spent evangelizing for every newly baptized member. When it is taken into consideration that this includes family members, the Witnesses are probably averaging over five thousand hours of door-to-door work for every single convert! Doing 204 hours of work

---

[20] Statistics posted to "Watchtower: Official Web Site of Jehovah's Witnesses" (*www.watchtower.org*).

per year in the field, this would mean the average Witness makes one convert every twenty-five years. As a result, it is not uncommon for a Witness to burn out and leave the organization. In fact, an ex-Witness noted another side of Watchtower statistics when he observed, "If Watchtower membership and baptismal statistics are analyzed over a ten-year period using their annual 'Yearbook' report, an incredible shortfall is revealed. In a typical ten-year period between 750,000 and 950,000 Witnesses leave the movement."[21]

Nonetheless, the evangelization efforts yielded a growth rate of 3.6 percent in 1998, with the baptism of 316,092 new members. As a result of such work, Witnesses can be found in 233 lands (countries or territories) in 87,644 congregations. While the Witnesses are to be commended for their constant efforts in evangelization, the fact remains that "they have a zeal for God; but not according to accurate knowledge" (Rom. 10:2).

Joining the Watchtower Organization

To those who are considering becoming Witnesses, the local Kingdom Hall is perhaps the friendliest five thousand square feet in their entire city. After initial contact with Witnesses and some return visits and Bible studies, prospective converts are invited there. They are given a great deal of attention, affirmation, and encouragement. This warm environment enables potential new members to develop a sense of belonging and often disarms them so that they may more easily trust the leader in his interpretation of Scripture.

When a Christian joins the Watchtower organization, it is often the case that he was never well grounded in the faith. Frequently, too, he comes from the ranks of the less educated. Often those who agree to participate in a Watchtower home Bible study have never attended any Bible study before, and for this reason

---

[21] Leonard and Marjorie Chretien, *Witnesses of Jehovah* (Eugene, Oregon: Harvest House Publishers, 1988), 15.

the number of conversions for the Witnesses is greatest where knowledge of the Bible is sparse.

After being invited to several Bible studies, Kingdom Hall meetings, and perhaps to tag along in door-to-door work, inquirers will be encouraged to join the "brothers and sisters" officially by means of baptism. They will then officially be "in the truth"—that is, keeping current with how Jehovah God is working through his organization. Because the impending Armageddon is always being stressed, inquirers tend to feel that the time is ripe to join the ranks of Jehovah's "faithful ones," making them eligible to live forever on earth when paradise is soon restored.

Once a member is baptized, however, it is not long before the honeymoon ends and he begins to feel like a number—someone used to gather more members and swell the ranks. In this regard, ex-Witnesses often confess that the Watchtower style of proselytizing felt to them like a pyramid business scheme, in which the efforts of large numbers of people are exploited for the benefit of a few at the top.

To intensify the motivation for proselytizing, the Watchtower has been using predictions of an impending Armageddon for over a century. This recurring theme of imminent heavenly warfare gives the Witnesses a sense of urgency about the need to get Jehovah's message out. The Watchtower's erroneous "end-times" dates and failed prophecies include 1874, 1878, 1914, 1915, 1918, 1925, 1943, and 1975. The employment of such tactics, though, has subsided and become less explicit in the past few decades because of the previous flawed predictions. Interestingly, Witnesses remain largely unaffected by the failed predictions, which the Watchtower explains away as "incomplete understandings" or overzealous interpretations of God's word. In fact, members are taught to laud the Watchtower for being up-front about its mistakes, for admitting its fallibility, and for seeking to understand better how biblical prophecies will eventually be fulfilled. In other words, the leadership ensures that the attention of the adherent is diverted from the issue of failed predictions to the issue of the Watchtower's integrity; and rather than seeing the Watchtower falsely claiming to speak for God, the Witnesses accept the "nobody's perfect" explanation.

A person considering joining the Watchtower is allowed to ask whatever questions come to mind, even if they challenge Watchtower theology. Once he becomes a baptized member, however, such critical thinking is to be laid to rest. Unquestioning loyalty is expected of the new member. He is led to believe that failure to remain obedient to the Watchtower and its teachings jeopardizes his eternal destiny. The Watchtower occasionally reminds its followers of their required loyalty to "God's organization":

> Are we assigned as individuals to bring forth the food for the spiritual table? No? Then let us not try to take over the slave's [the Watchtower's] duties. We should eat and digest and assimilate what is set before us, without shying away from parts of the food because it may not suit the fancy of our mental taste. The truths we are to publish are the ones provided through the discreet-slave-organization, not some personal opinions contrary to what that slave has provided as timely food.[22]

The Watchtower seeks to control the information to which its members have access. While many religious organizations do not wish the faithful to be exposed to what are regarded as false beliefs, the Watchtower is particularly adamant in this regard. For example, after explaining the thrill of Jehovah's promise to take away all pain and sorrow, bringing the faithful to live forever on a paradise earth with perfect health and complete happiness, one issue of *The Watchtower* mentions how this can all be lost by disobeying Jehovah by reading "apostate" literature: "What a terrible price to pay for . . . so-called independence!" Under the heading "Have No Dealings with Apostates" and across from the picture of the wise Witness trashing apostate literature, *The Watchtower* asks:

> Now, what will you do if you are confronted with apostate teaching—subtle reasonings—claiming that what you believe as one of

---

[22] *The Watchtower*, 1 February 1952, 79.

Jehovah's Witnesses is not the truth? For example, what will you do if you receive a letter or some literature, open it, and see right away that it is from an apostate? Will curiosity cause you to read it, just to see what he has to say? You may even reason: "It won't affect me; I'm too strong in the truth. And besides, if we have the truth, we have nothing to fear. The truth will stand the test." In thinking this way, some have fed their minds upon apostate reasoning and have fallen prey to serious questioning and doubt. . . . Tragically, others have gone back into complete darkness, even going back to Christendom's erroneous teachings.[23]

The article then goes on to say, that if Witnesses disregard the advice not to read such literature, they are disobeying Jehovah himself. Reading apostate literature is likened to looking at pornography, and Witnesses are told to avoid even the temptation to view apostate material: "Therefore, resolve in your heart that you will never even touch the poison that apostates want you to sip."[24] "Do you refuse to listen to bitter criticism of Jehovah's organization? You should refuse."[25]

In Watchtower literature, historical Christianity is labeled "apostate Christendom" and mainline Christian denominations are "spiritual fornicators" devoid of the guidance of Jehovah God. The Watchtower's view of all other denominations is summed up succinctly: "Outside the true Christian congregation [the Watchtower], what alternative organization is there? Only Satan's organization."[26]

Because of these considerations, Catholics attempting to share the truth with Witnesses typically find greater resistance than from members of other groups. Nevertheless, we are called by Christ to share the good news with everyone (Mark 16:15) in all its fullness (Matt. 28:20).

---

[23] Ibid., 15 March 1986, 11–13.

[24] Ibid., 20.

[25] Ibid., 15 May 1984, 17.

[26] Ibid., 1 March 1979, 24.

PART TWO

ANSWERING THE WATCHTOWER

(In the chapters of Part Two, Watchtower arguments are summarized and placed at the beginning of each chapter in italics.)

3

Should You Believe in the Trinity?

The idea of a Trinity is from Egyptian, Hindu, and pagan myths, inter-woven with Greek philosophy and borrowed from demonism. The Jewish Sh^ema' says, "God is one"—not three. The doctrine is false, unbiblical, and illogical.[1]

The doctrine of the Trinity, concisely defined, is that God is one divine Being who subsists in three divine Persons, known as the Father, the Son, and the Holy Spirit. In 1989, the Watchtower Bible and Tract Society published a 32-page booklet entitled *Should You Believe in the Trinity?* Predictably, the answer it gave was no.

This publication is a textbook example of a disingenuous and selective use of source materials. Its utility as a tool is limited by its audience's familiarity with the sources on which it draws. The more well read its readers are, the more its distortions and outright falsehoods will be exposed. Because so many have not had the chance to study the sources for themselves, the errors of this booklet should be exposed to show Witnesses that the Watchtower's presentation of the facts is not trustworthy.

One particular cue to this untrustworthiness is that the Watchtower's sources are difficult to check, since no footnotes are provided. Often a quote will be given without any reference as to its source. In response to inquiries by the present author and oth-

---

[1] See *Reasoning from the Scriptures* (Brooklyn: Watchtower Bible and Tract Society of New York, 1985), 405–26; *Should You Believe in the Trinity?* (Brooklyn: Watchtower Bible and Tract Society of New York, 1989), 32.

ers, the Watchtower has stated that the bibliographical informationwas omitted to save space, but when one reads the quotes in context, a more credible reason for the omission becomes obvious: It doesn't want adherents to check the booklet's sources. In numerous instances the sources cited actually say the exact opposite of what the reader is led to believe. But since the reader can only know this by seeing the context of the excerpts, it is not surprising that the Watchtower fails to provide bibliographical data.

The booklet presents several different kinds of arguments concerning the Trinity. Some are based on biblical texts, and some are historical or philosophical in nature. The arguments based on biblical texts will be dealt with in the next few chapters. This chapter examines the historical and philosophical arguments.

Historical Arguments

There are basically three historical objections Witnesses make to the doctrine of the Trinity: (1) that it is of pagan origin, (2) that it was not formulated until after Scripture had been completed, and (3) that the Church Fathers of the first three centuries did not believe in the Trinity.

Is the Trinity Pagan?

In *Should You Believe*, the Watchtower claims that the Egyptians worshiped a trinity, Osiris, Isis, and Horus—thousands of years before the Catholic Trinity. However, the Egyptians had many groupings of gods and goddesses—some in pairs, others in triads or much larger groups. The idea that the Egyptians had a trinity is simply false:

> The Egyptians had an Ennead—a pantheon of nine major gods and goddesses. Osiris, Isis, and Horus were simply three divinities in the pantheon who were closely related by marriage and blood (not surprising, since the Ennead itself was an extended family) and who

figured in the same myth cycle. They did not represent the three Persons of a single divine Being, the Christian idea of a Trinity.[2]

The Watchtower also lists the Hindus as having a triune godhead. However, there are literally hundreds of millions of Hindu gods. This extensive polytheism can hardly be used as evidence against the Trinity. It is true that Hindus often view their lesser deities as manifestations of three greater deities: Brahma (the creator), Vishnu (the preserver), and Shiva (the destroyer). These three deities are known in Hindu cosmogony as the *trimurti*, and they are said to have proceeded from the great world-egg that itself had been created by the First Cause. So again, while we may see a grouping of three deities, like the three junior members of the Ennead mentioned above, we do not see a single divine Being who has existed from all eternity in three Persons, which is what would be required to claim that a pagan religion believed in a Trinity.

Elsewhere in *Should You Believe*, quotes are taken from numerous individuals and presented as if these individuals denounced the Trinity as a pagan doctrine. Indeed, some of the authors the Watchtower quotes seem bent on finding connections to paganism everywhere and attribute to paganism a variety of doctrines and practices common to both Christians *and Jehovah's Witnesses*. These include baptism,[3] the Lord's Supper,[4] the Virgin Birth and the Nativity of Christ,[5] the Last Judgment,[6] and many others.[7] Witnesses cannot merely defer to the opinions of these individuals

---

[2] James Akin, "Chapter & Verse: The Pagan Influence Fallacy," *This Rock* (March 2000), 40.

[3] Arthur Weigall, *The Paganism in Our Christianity* (New York: G. P. Putnam's Sons, 1928), 134.

[4] Ibid., 146, 147.

[5] Ibid., 44, 47, 52, 60.

[6] Will Durant, *The Story of Civilization* (New York: Simon & Schuster, 1944), 3:595.

[7] See the *Encyclopedia of Anti-Trinitarian Deceptive Quoting*, currently located on-line at *www.bible.ca/trinity/trinity-jw-deceptions.htm*.

on what is and is not of pagan origin without undermining many of their own beliefs and practices.[8] Further, in the case of some individuals the Watchtower uses for support, the quotes are not represented correctly. The Watchtower does not provide the context from which the quotes were taken. Especially suspicious is its gambit of taking quotes from Catholic and Protestant sources in an attempt to cast doubt on the Trinity. For example, a Catholic or Protestant source is cited as saying that the doctrine of the Trinity is not found *explicitly* in Scripture, but it will fail to note that the same source goes on to say that the doctrine is found *implicitly* in Scripture. This leads to our next section.

Not Formulated until after Scripture Was Finished

A common Watchtower argument against the Trinity is that it is not explicitly presented in Scripture and was not explicitly formulated until after Scripture was written. These things are true. However, this does not mean that the doctrine of the Trinity is not true.

That the Trinity is not explicitly presented in Scripture in no way means that it is not *implicitly* present. Nor is there any requirement that it should be presented in all its fullness. This is especially clear when one considers the historical situation of the early Israelites. God indicated to them that they were to be monotheists even though they were surrounded polytheists. Making the break with polytheism was difficult for them, and so God chose at first to emphasize the oneness of his Being, only gradually disclosing to them that there is more than one Person in this divine unity.

God planted seeds of this truth within the Old Testament while he was at work establishing monotheism for the Jews to

---

[8] For a fuller discussion of the problems with making allegations concerning pagan origins, see James Akin, "The Pagan Influence Fallacy," *This Rock* (March 2000), 39–41; "Tracking the First Pagans," *This Rock* (November 1999, 38–39); and "The Woman, the Seed, the Serpent," *This Rock* (October 1999), 39–40.

set them apart from the believers of all the polytheistic religions that abounded. Monotheism was virtually unheard of in that age, and if God announced that he was one God in three Persons, the people would not have correctly understood him but would have embraced a notion of tritheism (the belief in or worshiping of three gods). God thus waited for the Christian era—*after* the threat of polytheism had been settled—to fully reveal his plurality of Persons.

This gradual disclosure of himself and his will, known to theologians as "progressive revelation," is obvious to all who read Scripture. Ideas that in the early books of the Old Testament are present, if at all, only in rudimentary form become major themes in the New Testament. God's revelation to the Jews was a gradual process. This is true even within the New Testament era itself. As Jesus said, "I have many things yet to say to you, but you are not able to bear them at present" (John 16:12).

Even human parents and teachers provide information to their children in graduated amounts, giving them as much as they can handle and digest; and the pace at which the child receives and assimilates the information depends on the child, not the parent. God, as a heavenly parent, operates in the same way. Like all good teachers, the Lord takes into account the capacity of his disciples at any given moment and leads them into the truth slowly, by planting seeds and letting the needed understanding grow and develop over the course of time.

Since God has used progressive revelation to communicate a variety of doctrines, it comes as no surprise that God would choose to reveal the most sublime and sophisticated teachings concerning himself only in stages. But even in the Old Testament, when the focus was still primarily on God's oneness of being, there are indications that there was still some form of plurality about the one Godhead.

Biblical examples of these seeds of the doctrine of the Trinity include the repeated references to God as "one." In Deuteronomy 6:4, for instance, one finds what is known as the *Sh^ema'*, the Jewish expression of monotheism: "Hear, O Israel: The LORD our

God is one LORD" (RSV:CE). There are two words in Hebrew for "one": *yachid*, meaning only one, something that is solitary or alone; and *'echad*, which can suggest a unity of several parts or things, as in Genesis: "evening and morning . . . one [*'echad*] day" or "husband and wife . . . one [*'echad*] flesh." It is the word *'echad* that is used in the *Sh^ema'* to speak of God. So the very foundation of monotheism, the Jewish *Sh^ema'*, hints at the idea of the Trinity without explicitly revealing it. God is not by essence a solitude, but a unity of three Persons—Father, Son, and Holy Spirit.

Other implicit references to the Trinity in the Old Testament include Genesis 1:26, which reads, "Let us make man in our image, according to our likeness." Since God was alone at the time of creation (Is. 44:24, Neh. 9:6), with no other gods, this plurality of persons refers to God himself. Again, at the Tower of Babel God says, "Let *us* go down," yet no one else comes down with him (Gen. 11:7). Despite these implicit references, it can be said without hesitation that the Jews did not have a full understanding of the Trinity, but many Jews—even before the time of Christ— recognized that Scripture hinted that there was more to the Godhead than a simple unitarianism would suggest.

In the New Testament, as we will see in coming chapters, the identities of the Persons of the Godhead are much more clearly set forth. Christ distinctly revealed that there are three Persons in the Godhead—the Father, the Son, and the Holy Spirit. Christ also revealed that God is love (1 John 4:16). But can love actually exist in isolation, as Witnesses suppose was the case before the creation of the world?

In order for love to exist, there must be a lover, a beloved, and the love between them. If God were a solitary Person, there would have been no love apart from the creation of the world, making God dependent on the world for part of his very nature. In 1 John 4:16, we are told that God *is* love, not merely that God *shows* love.) But by his nature, God cannot be dependent on the world for his essence as love, and so we see a plurality within the Godhead suggested: The Lover is the Father, his Beloved is the Son, and the Love between them is the Holy Spirit. The Trinity is an eternal union of love between these three divine Persons. Since all three have existed before time, they have existed from all eternity, and there was never a time when one did not exist.

What of the accusation that the term *Trinity* is not found in Scripture? To one familiar with apologetics, this is the weakest of all objections. When interpreting the Bible, every group inevitably creates its own theological vocabulary to describe concepts it perceives within Scripture. That these theological terms do not appear in the Bible is insignificant. Indeed, the very term *Bible* does not appear in the Bible! The Watchtower Bible and Tract Society is scarcely in a position to object to the Catholic Church's using a post-biblical term to describe what it perceives in Scripture, since the Watchtower itself does so. Some of its key terms, including *Governing Body, earthly class, generation of 1914,* and *disfellowshipping,* though not used in Scripture, are prominent in the Watchtower's theological literature. The real question is not "Is this *word* found in Scripture?" but "Is the *concept* behind this word found in Scripture?" As will be seen over the next few chapters, the concept of the Trinity *is.*

The Early Church Fathers and the Trinity

In its book *Qualified to Be Ministers,* the Watchtower advises its adherents to "be very careful to be accurate in all statements you make. Use evidence honestly. In quotations, do not twist the meaning of a writer or speaker or use only partial quotations to give a different thought than the person intended."[9]

This advice is disregarded in *Should You Believe.* Justin Martyr, Irenaeus, Clement of Alexandria, Tertullian, Hippolytus, and Origen are six early Christian writers quoted as favoring the Watchtower's unitarian doctrine of God, but complete documentation for its quotes is omitted. Why? Because each affirmed that Jesus was God, and several gave a detailed explanation of the Trinity. It

---

[9] *Qualified to Be Ministers* (Brooklyn: Watchtower Bible and Tract Society of New York, 1967), 199.

is also significant that Ignatius of Antioch (the apostle John's own disciple) is omitted from the list, for his letters refer seven times to Jesus as God.

The Watchtower admitted to the present author that its quotes from the Church Fathers were taken from *The Church of the First Three Centuries*, an obscure, out-of-print book, written in the mid-1800s by Alvan Lamson, a Unitarian. In a letter from the Watchtower to this author dated November 12, 1999, the Writing Department wrote, "Since this book was published back in 1869, we do not know what edition of the writings of the early Church Fathers that Lamson used." Despite this, in *Should You Believe* Lamson is quoted freely, noting that he claimed, "The modern popular doctrine of the Trinity . . . derives no support from the language of Justin [Martyr]: and this observation may be extended to all the ante-Nicene Fathers; that is, to all Christian writers for three centuries after the birth of Christ."[10] To respond to such a strong claim, one must go to the primary sources and discover what the Church Fathers actually said.

Should You Believe states that "Justin Martyr . . . called the pre-human Jesus a created angel." No citation is given for where Justin says this. There exist three complete writings from Justin Martyr, and in none of them does he refer to Jesus as a created angel. Justin Martyr calls Jesus "King, and Priest, and God, and Lord, and angel, and man, and captain, and stone, and a Son."[11] How can Justin declare Jesus to be both God and "an angel"? The solution is simple for anyone with a rudimentary knowledge of the Greek language. The Greek word for angel is *angelos*, which can also be translated "messenger"—and, indeed, Jesus can rightly be called a messenger who announces the Father's will, without himself ceasing to be God. That this is Justin's understanding is illustrated by the fact that he had previously referred to Jesus as "both God and Lord of hosts."[12] However, the Watchtower fails

---

[10] *Should You Believe,* 7 (ellipsis and brackets in original).

[11] *Dialogue with Trypho the Jew* 34.

[12] Ibid., 36.

to mention that Justin said this and relies on the translation of *angelos* as "angel" rather than "messenger" so that its idea of Jesus' not being God but rather Michael the archangel can appear to have some historical basis.

Other examples of Justin Martyr's espousing orthodox Catholic doctrine can be found in his *First Apology*, where he affirms in chapter 6 that Christians worship and adore the Father, the Son, and the Holy Spirit. In *Dialogue with Trypho the Jew*, he proclaims, "Therefore these words testify explicitly that he [Jesus] is witnessed to by him [the Father] who established these things, as deserving to be worshipped, as God and as Christ."[13]

Irenaeus is also cited as giving evidence against the Trinity, with the implication that he taught that Jesus was not equal to God. Again, no documentation is given. In a quote *not* used by the Watchtower, however, Irenaeus refers to "Jesus Christ our Lord and God and Savior and King."[14] His position is clear:

> For I have shown from the Scriptures, that no one of the sons of Adam is as to everything, and absolutely, called God, or named Lord. But that he is himself in his own right, beyond all men who ever lived, God, and Lord, and King Eternal, and the Incarnate Word, proclaimed by all the prophets, the apostles, and by the Spirit himself, may be seen by all who have attained to even a small portion of the truth.[15]

And what of Clement of Alexandria? Did he call Jesus "a creature" in his prehuman existence, as the Watchtower publication claims? Again no reference is given, since no such reference exists. Searching through all of Clement's extant writings, one discovers that he never uses this term in reference to Jesus. So where does the quote come from? It can be found in Lamson's *The Church of the First Three Centuries*, which explains that a ninth-century writer

---

[13] Ibid., 43.

[14] *Against Heresies* 1:10:1.

[15] Ibid., 3:19:2.

named Photius (the instigator of the Photian schism) charged Clement with making the Son "a creature."[16] The Watchtower thus asks us to believe that Clement made such a statement on the shaky authority of a nineteenth-century Unitarian (Lamson), citing a ninth-century schismatic (Photius), citing an unidentified source from five hundred years earlier that has never been found (Clement?). Such efforts give one the impression that the Watchtower is desperately groping for any evidence at all to support its doctrines.

Instead of quoting from this obscure document, the Watchtower would have done well to go to Clement's own easily obtained writings, in which this statement can be found:

> For "before the morning star it was" and "in the beginning was the Word, and the Word was with God, and the Word was God." . . . This Word, then, the Christ . . . this very Word has now appeared as man, he alone being both, both God and man. . . . The Word, who in the beginning bestowed on us life as Creator when he formed us, taught us to live well when he appeared as our Teacher; that as God he might afterwards conduct us to the life which never ends.[17]

Another writer to have had his writings subverted is Tertullian. The Watchtower argues that he says, "There was a time when the Son was not." In his *Against Hermogenes* (chap. 3), Tertullian does say that there was a time when the Son did not exist with the Father. But the Watchtower again omits an important fact. Tertullian affirms that the Word of God is eternal with the First and Third Persons of the Trinity, but he thinks that the *Word* of God did not become the *Son* of God until the Incarnation. That's why he says that there was a time when the Son was not. This is a theological error, but it lends no patristic support to the idea that Jesus is not God. It should also be noted that Tertullian was the

---

[16] Alvan Lamson, *The Church of the First Three Centuries* (Boston: Horace B. Fuller, 1869), 124.

[17] *Exhortation to the Heathen* 1.

first to employ the use of the Latin word *Trinitas* ("Trinity") to explain the nature of God.[18]

What does Tertullian have to say for himself? The following excerpts clarify what he thought about the Trinity:

Him we believe to have been sent by the Father into the Virgin, and to have been born of her—being both Man and God, the Son of Man and the Son of God, and to have been called by the name of Jesus Christ . . . while the mystery of the dispensation is still guarded, which distributes the Unity into a Trinity, placing them in their order the three Persons—the Father, the Son, and the Holy Ghost.[19]

It was because he [the Father] had already his Son close at his side— as a second Person, his own Word—and a third Person also—the Spirit in the Word—that [in Genesis 1–3] he purposely adopted the plural phrase, "Let us make;" and, "in our image;" and, "become as one of us." . . . With these did he then speak, in the Unity of the Trinity. . . . I mean the Word of God, "through whom all things were made, and without whom nothing was made." Now if he, too, is God, according to John, (who says,) "The Word was God," then you have two Beings—One that commands that the thing be made, and the Other that executes the order and creates. In what sense, however, you ought to understand him to be another. I have already explained, on the ground of Personality, not of Substance —in the way of distinction, not of division.[20]

Thus the connection of the Father in the Son, and of the Son in the Paraclete, produces three coherent Persons, who are yet distinct One from Another. These Three are one essence, not one Person, as it is said, "I and my Father are One" [John 10:30], in respect of unity of Being not singularity of number.[21]

---

[18] The Greek word *trias* had already been in use for some time, being first recorded in the writings of Theophilus of Antioch, c. A.D. 180.

[19] *Against Praxeas*, 2.

[20] Ibid., 12.

[21] Ibid., 25.

Next comes Hippolytus, who is claimed to have affirmed that God is one and that there was nothing before him—"such as the created prehuman Jesus," the anonymous Watchtower author adds. The Catholic Church agrees that God is one and that there was nothing before him, but is the additional commentary by the Watchtower reliable? Hippolytus says the following:

> For Christ is the God above all, and he has arranged to wash away sin from human beings.
> The Word alone of this God is from God himself, wherefore also the Word is God, being the Being of God. Now the world was made from nothing, wherefore it is not God.[22]

Lastly, Origen is also said by the Watchtower to have had no knowledge of the Trinity. But the following passages demonstrate the unreliability of this claim. In the first of them, Origen explicitly condemns the idea that Jesus is a created being:

> For *we do not hold that which the heretics imagine*: that some part of the Being of God was converted into the Son, or that the Son was procreated by the Father from non-existent substances, that is, from a Being outside himself, so *that there were a time when he [the Son] did not exist*.
> No, rejecting every suggestion of corporeality, we hold that the Word and the Wisdom was begotten out of the invisible and incorporeal God, without anything corporal being acted upon . . . the expression which we employ, however that there was never a time when he did not exist is to be taken with a certain allowance. For these very words "when" and "never" are terms of temporal significance, while whatever is said of the Father, the Son, and the Holy Spirit, is to be understood as transcending all time, all ages, and all eternity.
> From all which we learn that the person of the Holy Spirit was of such authority and dignity, that saving baptism was not complete except by the authority of the most excellent Trinity.
> For it is one and the same thing to have a share in the Holy Spirit, which is (the Spirit) of the Father and the Son, since the nature of the Trinity is one and incorporeal.

---

[22] *The Refutation of All Heresies* (*Philosophumena*), 10:30, 29.

> Although he was God, he took flesh; and having been made man, he remained what he was: God.[23]

After reading through this sampling of quotes from the first three centuries, can the Watchtower be considered a trustworthy authority when, quoting Lamson, it says, "The modern popular doctrine of the Trinity . . . derives no support from . . . all Christian writers for three centuries after the birth of Christ"?[24] It would not seem so. There is abundant evidence for belief in the Trinity in the documents of the first three centuries.

Philosophical Objections

Among the philosophical objections Witnesses commonly make regarding the Trinity, the most prominent concerns a confusion between the existence of three divine Persons and three gods. Witnesses may ask, "If there are three divine persons, aren't there three gods?" Here one must understand the difference between being and person, for these are two distinct things.

Informally speaking, we could say something's "being" addresses the question "What?"—the kind of thing it is—while "person" answers the question "Who?" For example, about my mother, the question "What is she?" could be answered "A human being." The question "Who is she?" is answered "Janie." All persons are beings, but not all beings are persons. For example, a rock is not a person, though it is a being. With regard to the Trinity, there is one Being, which is God, yet this Being is three Persons: the Father, the Son, and the Holy Spirit. This is not illogical. If one were to say that there is one God and three gods, or one Person and three Persons—that *would* be illogical.

But, "one Being and three Persons" is not a contradiction, since oneness and threeness are being applied to God in two *different* ways. In one way, God is one (one Being), but in another he is

---

[23] *The Fundamental Doctrines (De Principiis)*, 4:1:28 (emphases added); 1:3:2; 4:1:32, 4 (preface).
[24] *Should You Believe*, 7.

three (three Persons). The logical coherence of this cannot be denied on the grounds that it transcends our experience to find one being who is more than one person. First, God himself transcends our experience and, as the greatest Being that exists, it should not be surprising that he has aspects that are unlike what we have experienced here on earth. That would only be expected.

Second, logic alone shows that if there can be beings that are less than one person (e.g., a rock) and beings that are exactly one person (e.g., a human), then there is no identification or necessary one-to-one correlation between being and person; so there is no reason one cannot have a being that is more than one person (e.g., God). A Witness may not like this, but there is nothing illogical or contradictory about it.

This is not to say that Witnesses will not characterize it as such. Indeed, one of their favorite tactics is to cite Christians referring to the Trinity as a mystery:

> Cardinal John O'Connor states: "We know that it is a very profound mystery, which we don't begin to understand." And Pope John Paul II speaks of "the inscrutable mystery of God the Trinity."[25]

Though no sources are given, we should not be surprised at finding two such churchmen describing the Trinity in such terms, for the Trinity *is* a mystery—and that is nothing to be ashamed of. Indeed, the New Testament itself refers to various divinely revealed mysteries. The 1910 *Catholic Encyclopedia* explains in its article "Mystery":

> In the New Testament the word mystery is applied ordinarily to the sublime revelation of the gospel [Matt. 13:11; Col. 2:2; 1 Tim. 3:9; 1 Cor. 15:51], and to the Incarnation and life of the Saviour and his manifestation by the preaching of the apostles [Rom. 16:25; Eph. 3:4; 6:19; Col. 1:26; 4:3].
>
> In conformity with the usage of the inspired writers of the New Testament, theologians give the name mystery to revealed truths

---

[25] Ibid., 4.

that surpass the powers of natural reason. Mystery, therefore, in its strict theological sense is not synonymous with the incomprehensible, since all that we know is incomprehensible, i.e., not adequately comprehensible as to its inner being; nor with the unknowable, since many things merely natural are accidentally unknowable, on account of their inaccessibility, e.g., things that are future, remote, or hidden. In its strict sense a mystery is a supernatural truth, one that of its very nature lies above the finite intelligence.

Theologians distinguish two classes of supernatural mysteries: the absolute (or theological) and the relative. An absolute mystery is a truth whose existence or possibility could not be discovered by a creature, and whose essence (inner substantial being) can be expressed by the finite mind only in terms of analogy, e.g., the Trinity. A relative mystery is a truth whose innermost nature alone (e.g., many of the divine attributes), or whose existence alone (e.g., the positive ceremonial precepts of the Old Law), exceeds the natural knowing power of the creature.

The Trinity is a mystery in that it is something about God that could not be deduced without his having revealed the fact to us, as he does in sacred Scripture. It is also a mystery in that its innermost nature can only be understood by our limited minds by way of analogy. It is no surprise, then, when we find churchmen such as the late Cardinal O'Connor or Pope John Paul II adverting to the mysterious nature of the Trinity.

There are many mysteries, even of the natural order, that have the character of being understandable only by analogy. For example, when we contemplate the atomic structure of matter, we often imagine subatomic particles, such as electrons, protons, and neutrons, as if they were tiny spheres that relate to each other in certain ways—but they aren't actually like that. This is just a model, an analogy to help us understand what is taking place on a subatomic level. Our minds have not fully penetrated the nature of matter; much less have they fully penetrated the nature of God.

Indeed, given how far God is above us in the order of being, we never will fully penetrate the mystery of God. He is infinite; our minds are finite. There must always remain that about God which is mysterious to us—that which we could not have learned about him without revelation and cannot fully penetrate even when it is revealed to us. For Witnesses to deny this would be to imagine a god about whom everything could be deduced and comprehended by the finite human mind, a god who is himself finite—thus unworthy of worship.

On the subject of God's transcendence of man's understanding, Scripture is clear:

> "For the thoughts of you people are not my thoughts, nor are my ways your ways," is the utterance of Jehovah. "For as the heavens are higher than the earth, so my ways are higher than your ways, and my thoughts than your thoughts." (Is. 55:8–9)

> O the depth of God's riches and wisdom and knowledge! How unsearchable his judgments [are] and past tracing out his ways [are]! For "who has come to know Jehovah's mind, or who has been his counselor?" Or, "Who has first given to him, so that it might be repaid to him? Because from him and by him and for him are all things." (Rom. 11:33–35, citing Is. 40:13, Job 41:11)

∼

What is to be learned from this investigation of *Should You Believe in the Trinity?* Is one to conclude that Witnesses willingly seek to deceive as many people as possible? Hardly. But the vast majority of Witnesses have probably never read a page of the Church Fathers as such or consulted an encyclopedia of mythology. They would not even know where to begin to look for them.

Witnesses tend to be very sincere people who strive to know and follow God, but their biggest and most tragic error is that they have placed their complete trust in an authority that deserves none at all. The Watchtower is guilty of irresponsible and sloppy research, and the victims are the unsuspecting readers. These Witnesses know well from their reading of Scripture that there is an authority instituted by Christ to guide them. Whoever hears it should be hearing Christ (Luke 10:16). They know that Scripture commands them to obey and submit to leaders within the Church

(Heb. 13:17) and that the Church is the "pillar and support of the truth" (1 Tim. 3:15). Unfortunately, they have not made the correct identification of that Church. With all love, they must be invited back to that One, Holy, Catholic, and Apostolic Church.

4

Is Jesus Michael the Archangel?

1 Thessalonians 4:16 says that Jesus "will descend from heaven with a commanding call, with an archangel's voice and with God's trumpet." So, if Jesus has the voice of an archangel, he must be the archangel Michael. After all, Michael is the only archangel there is, since the term archangel is never used in the plural. Thus the evidence indicates that Jesus is the firstborn of all creation (Col. 1:15) and was known as Michael before he came to earth, and he is again known by the name Michael since his return to heaven.[1]

Perhaps the most peculiar Watchtower doctrine is the idea that Jesus is really Michael the archangel. This teaching is not typically mentioned when introducing the faith to a new recruit, as can be seen in the official overview of beliefs published by the Watchtower. If Witnesses have difficulty explaining any particular doctrine, it is this one. They openly admit that if one were to walk up to any of the twelve apostles and ask who Jesus was, none would have said, "But of course, he's Michael the archangel!"

The clearest contradiction of such an idea can be found in the book of Hebrews (RSV:CE), where the sacred author asks, "For to what angel did God ever say, 'Thou art my Son' "? (1:5, citing Ps. 2:7,) and "When he brings the first-born into the world, he says, 'Let all God's angels worship him' " (1:6, citing Deut. 32:43). "Of the angels he says, 'Who makes his angels winds, and his servants flames of fire.' But of the Son he says, 'Thy throne,

---

[1] *Reasoning from the Scriptures* (Brooklyn: Watchtower Tract and Bible Society of New York, 1985), 218.

O God, is for ever and ever . . .' and, 'Thou, Lord, didst found the earth in the beginning, and the heavens are the work of thy hands' " (1:7–8, citing Ps. 104:4, 45:6, and 102:25).

Here the author of Hebrews not only separates Jesus from angels, he even commands the angels to worship him (Heb. 1:6; cf. Rev. 5:13–14, 14:7). The first issue of *Zion's Watch Tower* magazine agreed: " 'Let *all* the angels of God worship him' [that must include Michael] and 'Thy throne, O God, is forever and ever.' "[2] The obvious problem, though, is this: Archangels are creatures, but the Bible forbids the worship of any created being. Thus, either the Bible is in error by commanding the angels to worship an archangel, or Jesus is uncreated, deserving of worship, and cannot be an archangel.

In Revelation 22:8–9 an angel refuses to be worshiped, but God the Father commands that the same worship (Greek, *proskuneō*) be given to Jesus (Heb. 1:6). Since this proved to be a stumbling block for Watchtower theology, the NWT had to be altered to eliminate the references to Christ's being worshiped. The translation of *proskuneō* was therefore changed to read "do obeisance" when in reference to Christ, but it was left as "worship" when speaking of Jehovah. So Hebrews 1:6, 8 in the NWT now reads, " 'And let all of God's angels do obeisance to him.' . . . 'God is your throne forever.' "[3]

Michael the archangel's name is mentioned only five times in Scripture: in Daniel 10:13, 21; 12:1; Jude 9; and Revelation 12:7. He is described as "one of the foremost princes," who "did not dare to bring a judgment against him [Satan] in abusive terms, but said: 'May Jehovah rebuke you.' " Jesus, like Jehovah, never seemed to have any qualms about rebuking Satan, since he did

---

[2] *Watchtower Reprints*, 9 (*Zion's Watch Tower*, July 1879, 9; brackets and italics in original text).

[3] The 1953, 1960, 1961, and 1970 editions of the NWT render *proskuneō* in Heb. 1:6 as "worship" rather than "do obeisance."

this dozens of times in the Gospels.[4] More importantly, Jesus has the power to forgive sins and give eternal life, but no angel has this capacity.

Since Michael is called "*the* archangel" in Jude 9 (emphasis added), is one to conclude that he is the *only* archangel, as the Watchtower asserts? Such reasoning would lead one to believe that the title "Felix *the* cat" implies that there are no other cats but Felix. Such a use of the definite article *the* obviously does not at all mean that there are no others. In addition, Michael is only considered to be "*one* of the foremost princes" (Dan. 10:13, emphasis added). This implies that there are more princes like him. In contrast to Michael, Jesus is called "King of kings and Lord of lords" (Rev. 19:13, 16). He is not simply one among many princes.

The Watchtower not only attempts to equate Jesus with Michael; it also tries to buttress its argument that Jesus is a creature (an archangel, no matter how exalted, is still merely a creature) by appealing to Colossians 1:15, where he is called "the firstborn of creation." What about this argument? Does the phrase "firstborn of creation" imply that Jesus was created? In the case of Colossians 1:15, the Greek word for "firstborn" is *prōtotokos*, which can mean either a firstborn in chronological birth order or one who is preeminent. To see this difference in meaning, compare Genesis 41:51–52 ("Joseph called the name of the firstborn Manasseh . . . the name of the second he called Ephraim") with Jeremiah 31:9 ("I have become to Israel a Father; and as for Ephraim, he is my firstborn").

In these verses, *firstborn* has two different meanings, since Ephraim is considered firstborn, although he was not first to leave the womb. Therefore, the use of the term *firstborn* in reference to Jesus does not at all mean that he is a created being but rather that he is preeminent over creation. There is also something to say about the *of* in the phrase "firstborn of all creation." The *of* is present in the English because in Greek the words *all creation*

---

[4] Compare Jude 9 with Luke 4:41.

(*pasēs ktiseōs*) are in the genitive case.[5] When translators encounter
something in the genitive case in Greek, a standard way to translate it into English is to stick the word *of* in front of it. Of is
an English preposition that has a very broad range of meaning. It
can show possession (the genitive's best-known function), as in
"That is the house of John," but it can also show other things,
such as relationship, as in "That is the brother of John." And it
can show many other things as well.

In Colossians 1:15, the Jehovah's Witnesses are taking the genitive phrase "of all creation" to indicate a larger whole (the created
world) of which the Son is a part.[6] However, there are other kinds
of genitives. One shows primacy over something.[7] This seems to
be the kind of genitive used here. The passage is stressing Jesus'

---

[5] In Greek, nouns and adjectives take different forms depending on their
grammatical function in a sentence. When a Greek noun or adjective is in a
particular form, it is said to be in a particular "case." By figuring out its case,
you know something about its function. For example, if a particular noun is
serving as the subject of a sentence, its form will show this, and a Greek gram-
marian would say that it is in the "nominative" case (the nominative case's
best-known function is to tell us what the subject is).

This concept may be unfamiliar to many English-speakers. In English we use
case far less often than Greek does. We tend to use word order (e.g., putting
the subject prior to the verb) and "helper" words (e.g., *of, to*) to convey the
same information. However, we do use case sometimes, as with personal pro-
nouns. For example, *he, his,* and *him* are three forms of the same English word,
and their form tells what function they are performing. If you see a *he*, it's a
subject. If you see a *his*, it's a possessive. And if you see a *him*, it's an object.
Thus "He hit his baseball" and "His baseball hit him" mean two different
things. It isn't only the word order that tells you this; it is also the shift between
he and *him*.

[6] The fancy name for this is the *partitive genitive*, since it presents something
as *part* of a larger whole.

[7] This has been called the genitive of primacy (and, curiously, as the genitive
of subordination). Biblical examples include "King of Israel" (Mark 15:32),
"God of this people of Israel" (Acts 13:17), "King of saints" (Rev. 15:3) —
see Daniel B. Wallace, *Greek Grammar Beyond the Basics* (Grand Rapids: Zondervan, 1997), 103–4.

primacy over all things, which verses 16 and 17 say were created through and for the Son and that he is what holds them together, putting him in a category different from and superior to the created world).[8] This makes it more plausible to translate the phrase "the firstborn *over* all creation."

---

[8] This is a real problem for the Watchtower. The phrase "all things" occurs five times in Col. 1:16–20, and to prevent the text from placing Jesus in a different, uncreated class, the NWT inserts the word *other* into the phrase to create an exception for the Son. Thus it says that "by means of him all [other] things were created," and "All [other] things have been created through him and for him," etc. This exception is not in the Greek. Indeed, the Greek has only a single word corresponding to "all things"—*panta*, which would literally be translated "all." To avoid this in its translation, the Watchtower repeatedly inserts a word to get around the plain meaning of the text. (A similar problem text for them is John 1:3, which states that "all things were made through him, and without him was not anything made that was made" [RSV:CE]).

5

Is Jesus God?

Jesus is the Son of God, the firstborn of all creation. He was the first one created by Jehovah God, and it was by means of him that the Father created all other things. Jesus often prayed to God, so it is clear that he is not God. A correct translation of John 1:1 testifies to this fact: "In the beginning the Word was, and the Word was with God, and the Word was a god." Jesus knew who he was, and he so admitted, "The Father is greater than I." Only the Father is God, which in Greek is ho Theos. Jesus may be a mighty god, but only Jehovah is almighty God.[1]

Who created the world, forgives sins, gives eternal life, and is worthy to receive worship? If you answer that a creature could do all of these, you would be radically departing from orthodox Christian teaching. If you assert that Jesus could not do these, you contradict Scripture.[2] For that reason, the doctrine that most clearly sets the Witnesses apart from Christians is their denial of the divinity of Christ. The Bible is replete with evidence proclaiming that Jesus is God, and one doesn't need a Ph.D. in theology to remember a few of the passages.

The Word Was God (John 1:1)

John 1:1 states unequivocally, "In the beginning was the Word, and the Word was with God, and *the Word was God*" (RSV:CE;

---

[1] *Reasoning from the Scriptures* (Brooklyn: Watchtower Bible and Tract Society of New York, 1985), 209−18.

[2] See Heb. 1:10, Mark 2:57, John 10:28, and Rev. 5:13−14.

emphasis added). This verse understandably has caused Witnesses tremendous difficulty. As with numerous other Bible passages, the Watchtower doctored this one so that it could be reconciled with Watchtower theology, arguing that Greek sentence structure and proper grammar require that the English indefinite article *a* be placed before the word *God* (*theos*). The NWT now reads, "and the word was *a* god" (emphasis added). We take an in-depth look at this translation error in the chapter "Can You Trust the *New World Translation*?" In the present chapter other arguments concerning the divinity of Christ are examined.

My Lord and My God! (John 20:28)

In John 20:28 Thomas says to Jesus, "My Lord and my God," which in the Greek is "*Ho Kurios mou kai ho Theos mou.*" Translated literally, the sentence reads, "The Lord of me and the God of me." It would be nothing short of blasphemy for Jesus not to rebuke Thomas if he were wrong.[3] Jesus does nothing of the sort, but in fact he accepts Thomas's profession of faith that he is God in the next verse: "Because you have seen me have you believed? Happy are those who do not see and yet believe."

This is especially significant because the Watchtower teaches that the Greek phrase *ho Theos* ("the God") is used in Scripture to refer to the true God, as opposed to lesser gods. Yet here *ho Theos* is applied directly to Jesus, showing on the Watchtower's own logic that Jesus is *the* God, and not just *a* god. This creates a major theological problem for the Watchtower. To try to explain this verse, the claim is made that Thomas's statement was merely an exclamatory expression of praise directed to the Father. Yet the Watchtower's own NWT refutes this notion, as this verse clearly states that Thomas directed his words to Jesus: "In answer, Thomas said *to him*, 'My Lord and my God!' " (emphasis added).

---

[3] Indeed, not long afterward, King Herod Agrippa was struck dead following a failure to rebuke a divine accolade. See Acts 12:21–23.

God the Creator (Hebrews 1:10)

Psalm 102:24–25 reads, "O my God . . . Your years are throughout all generations. Long ago you laid the foundations of the earth itself. And the heavens are the work of your hands." Ask any Witness, "Who are these verses talking about?" Witnesses unanimously assert that they are speaking of Jehovah. And they are right. Verses 1, 12, 15, 16, 18, 19, 21, and 22 all make it clear —by using the divine name—that the God in question is indeed Jehovah.

However, the author of Hebrews takes the Psalmist's words and applies them to Jesus: "But with reference to the Son . . . 'You at [the] beginning O Lord, laid the foundations of the earth itself, and the heavens are [the] works of your hands" (1:8, 10). This single passage in Hebrews suffices to prove that Jesus is God— Jehovah—since an Old Testament reference to God is now applied to him.

Further, according to John 1:3 and Colossians 1:16–17, Jesus created the heavens and the earth, and yet Scripture is clear that God alone is the creator of the universe (Job 9:8, Is. 44:24, Neh. 9:6) and "he that constructed all things is God" (Heb. 3:4). The only way to reconcile these passages is to acknowledge that Jesus is God. In contrast to this, the Watchtower maintains that Jehovah created only one thing, and that was Michael the archangel. Then, this archangel supposedly created all *other* things.[4] Did God really make an archangel and then use him to create the rest of the universe? If so, the above-mentioned verses are in error in saying that God *alone* was the creator—and error cannot be attributed to inspired Scripture.

As was stated previously, Michael the archangel is mentioned five times in Scripture,[5] and not one of these passages is in refer-

---

[4] *United in Worship of the Only True God* (Brooklyn: Watchtower Bible and Tract Society of New York, 1983), 29.

[5] Dan. 10:13; 21; 12:1; Jude 9, Rev. 12:7.

ence to creation. Michael, then, stands in stark contrast to Jesus, for "apart from him *not even one thing* came into existence" (John 1:3, emphasis added).

I AM (John 8:58)

In John 8:58, Jesus takes the sacred name of God, "I AM" (from Ex. 3:14), and applies it to himself: "Amen, amen, I say to you, before Abraham came to be, I AM" (NAB). Only God may use this title of himself without blaspheming (Ex. 20:7, Deut. 5:11), and the punishment for misusing his name is death by stoning (Lev. 24:16). Thus Jesus' Jewish audience immediately recognized Jesus' claim to divinity and picked up stones to kill him (John 8:59).

This verse, like many others, has proved to be difficult for the Witnesses to combat, so in their NWT they have changed "I AM" to "I have been" to tone it down. The result is that they eliminated Jesus' claim of equality with God by applying the sacred name to himself. According to the Watchtower, "I have been" is a legitimate translation, being in the "perfect tense."[6]

The absurdity of the NWT translation is made manifest when one realizes that the Greek phrase it renders as "I have been" is *egō eimi*. This is the same phrase used in the Greek Old Testament when God appears to Moses in the burning bush and declares his name (Ex. 3:14). It is also one of the simplest phrases to translate from Greek. *Egō* is the Greek word for "I." It is the first personal pronoun that students of Greek language learn. *Eimi* is the first person present tense form of the verb *to be*. *Eimi* is typically the first form of the first verb that students of Greek learn. It

---

[6] Over the years, the Watchtower has said in the footnotes for John 8:58 in its NWT and its *Kingdom Interlinear Translation* (KIT) that the expression rendered "I have been" is (1) in the "perfect tense indicative" (1963, large print edition); (2) in the "perfect tense" (1969, KIT); and (3) in the "perfect indicative" (1985, KIT, revised edition). Though the specific designation varies from one footnote to another, all ascribe the Greek expression to the perfect tense (*indicative* refers to its mood rather than its tense).

means "am." There is probably no two-word, subject-verb phrase in Greek that is easier to translate than *egō eimi*. Even the least accomplished beginning Greek student who knows his first person pronoun and his verb *to be* in Greek can tell in a heartbeat that *egō eimi* is translated "I am."[7]

It should also be noted that it would be rather strange—even contrary to the Mosaic Law—for the Jews to stone Jesus for saying that he "had been." While such words may have sounded odd, there is nothing inherently blasphemous about them. Besides blasphemy, there were other acts that were punishable by stoning under the Mosaic Law, such as acting as a medium or fortune-teller (Lev. 20:27), false prophesying (Deut. 18:20), leading others to idolatry (Deut. 13:5–10), offering children to Molech (Lev. 20:2), being a rebellious and stubborn son (Deut. 21:18–21), and certain forms of sexual immorality (Deut. 22:21–24). Jesus was not guilty of any of these, and there is no question that the Jews were about to stone him for anything other than blasphemy.

Worship Him (Revelation 5:13–14; Hebrews 1:6)

While it is a sin to worship any creature (Rom. 1:25)—including angels (Rev. 22:8–9)—the Bible repeatedly proclaims that Jesus is to be worshiped.[8] Because the Watchtower claims that Jesus is an angelic creature, Revelation 22:8–9 is of primary importance, since it records an angel's refusing to be worshiped by John: "I fell down to worship before the feet of the angel. . . . But he tells me: 'Be careful! Do not do that! All I am is a fellow slave. . . . Worship God.'" In this passage, the Greek words for worship are *proskunēsai* and *proskunēson*. Turning to Hebrews 1:6, God commands, "And let all God's angels *proskunēsatōsan* him [Jesus]." So the worship that the angel refuses and commands that God be

---

[7] Incidentally, the perfect tense form of the verb *to be* does not even appear in the Greek New Testament, so there is no perfect tense equivalent of *egō eimi* appearing in its pages.

[8] See Matt. 28:17; Heb. 1:6; Rev. 5:13–14, 14:7, 22:3.

given is the same worship that the Father commands the angels to give to Jesus. The Son is given the same worship as that given to the Father (Rev. 5:13–14), since the Bible testifies that they have the same glory (John 17:5; 5:23; Rev. 5:11–14).

The Fullness of God (Colossians 2:9; cf. 1:19)

In a passage that is often overlooked by Witnesses, the New World Translation has St. Paul stating, "It is in him [Christ] that all the fullness of the divine quality dwells bodily" (Col. 2:9). Note that it is not fifty or ninety-five percent of the divine quality that dwells in Christ but the *fullness* of it. In other words, nothing of the divine nature is lacking in the person of Jesus Christ.

It should be mentioned that the Greek word here translated in the NWT as "divine quality" is *theotētos*, which actually means "divinity." This is a subtle difference but one with major implications. "Divine quality" makes Jesus merely God-*like*, whereas "divinity" makes Jesus God.[9] But once again, the Watchtower deliberately has mistranslated the Greek to fit its doctrine better.

Equal to God (John 5:18)

In John 5:18 one reads that Jesus "was also calling God his own Father, making himself equal to God." Note that John is not simply reporting what the Jews thought but stating that Jesus made himself equal to God.

Pray to Him (Acts 7:59)

Jehovah's Witnesses maintain that only Jehovah God may be prayed to. Since, in Acts 7:59, Stephen prays, "Lord Jesus, re-

---

[9] In support of this distinction, Kittel's *Theological Dictionary of the New Testament* provides only two possible definitions of the term *theotētos*: "divinity" or "Godhead;" cf. Gerhard Kittel, ed. (Grand Rapids: Eerdmans, 1965), 3:119.

ceive my spirit," one can only conclude by the Watchtower's reasoning that Jesus is God. Otherwise, Stephen blasphemes while filled with the Holy Spirit (7:55). Now the Watchtower tries to deflect the implication of this passage by saying that Stephen was not really praying but, instead, directly addressing Jesus in a vision:

> "But," some may ask, "does the Bible not report that both the disciple Stephen and the apostle John spoke to Jesus in heaven?" That is true. These events, however, did not involve prayers, as Stephen and John each saw Jesus in vision and spoke to him directly. (Acts 7:56, 59; Rev. 1:17–19; 22:20) [10]

At first glance this reasoning seems sound, but upon closer examination this interpretation of the passage falls apart. It is true that Stephen beholds a vision in verse 55, but then in verse 58 the angry crowd takes Stephen out of the city to stone him. He is no longer experiencing the vision.

But what about the assertion that Stephen was not actually praying to Jesus? Again, a closer look at the passage shows this to be untrue. The vision occurred in verse 55, and now at verse 58—in another place and under different conditions—Stephen is making a *petition* to Jesus to receive his spirit and to forgive those who are stoning him. This petition is almost identical to Jesus' prayer to the Father while on the cross: "Father, into your hands I entrust my spirit" (Luke 23:46). Further, Stephen identifies his heavenly savior as Jesus—*not* as Michael the archangel—again showing the perpetuity of the Incarnation.

Jesus Is Jehovah! (Romans 10:13, Revelation 2:23)

The NWT translates the Greek word for Lord (*Kurios*) as "Jehovah" throughout the New Testament whenever it designates God the Father, but it leaves the translation as "Lord" when the term is applied to Jesus. If it were consistent in translating *Kurios*

---

[10] *The Watchtower*, 15 December 1994, 24.

as "Jehovah," verses such as Philippians 2:11 would read, "and every tongue should confess that *Jesus Christ is Jehovah* to the glory of God the Father."

In Romans 10:13, Paul states that "every one who calls upon the name of the Lord will be saved" (RSV:CE). The NWT renders this passage, "For 'everyone who calls on the name of Jehovah will be saved.' " However, when this verse is read in the context of the prior four verses, it becomes very clear that Jesus is then Jehovah, since he is the Lord being spoken of.

Jeremiah 17:10 provides another example: "I, Jehovah, am searching the heart, examining the kidneys, even to give to each one according to his ways, according to the fruitage of his dealings." In Revelation 2:23, though, Jesus says, "I am he who searches the kidneys and hearts, and I will give you individually according to your deeds." So once again Jesus applies to himself the very words of Jehovah; thus, he is Jehovah.

How Could Jesus Be God If . . .

Upon providing the biblical evidence for the divinity of Christ, the Christian should be prepared to hear a litany of objections from the Witnesses, all beginning with, "How could Jesus be God if . . . " Below are the most popular ones (in italics), followed by material you can use to respond to their objections. Keep in mind that this is by no means an exhaustive list.

How could Jesus be God if he died? Who was running the universe for the three days he was in the tomb?

Here the Witnesses' doctrine of God is being colored by their understanding of what death is. For if death means unconsciousness or annihilation, then if Jesus died he certainly could not be God. To address this, it is necessary to explain that death is the separation of the body and the soul, not the annihilation of the person (see chapter 12 on the soul). Since Jesus did not cease being conscious after his human body died, it was no difficulty for him to "run the universe." After all, Hebrews 1:3 states that "he sustains all things by the word of his power."

How could Jesus be God if he does not "know the day or the hour," while the Father does (Matt. 24:36; Mark 13:32)?

The whole of Scripture must be taken into account so that individual passages are not considered in isolation from the rest, lest a faulty interpretation occur. This problem occurs when one reads *only* that Jesus doesn't know something that the Father does. Other portions of Scripture, such as John 16:30 and 21:17, make it clear that Jesus does not know everything. So in order to reconcile passages where Jesus *seems* not to know something with passages where he knows all, one must necessarily make a distinction between Christ's human nature and his divine nature. In other words, when Jesus seemingly doesn't know something, it is because he is speaking from his limited human nature; contrarily, when he "knows everything," he is speaking from his divine nature.

Furthermore, the Watchtower concedes a similar point in its own Bible dictionary, where it says of Jehovah, "God could choose not to foreknow indiscriminately all the future acts of his creatures."[11] It would seem inconsistent of Witnesses to expect the human mind of Jesus to foreknow all future events when they admit that, based on their conception of God, the divine mind itself could choose not to know all future events.[12]

How could Jesus be God if he is the mediator between God and man (1 Tim. 2:5)? A mediator stands between two parties and so can't be one of the parties.

If that argument were sound, then Christ could not be a man either. Yet Scripture calls him "a man, Christ Jesus" (1 Tim. 2:5),

---

[11] *Insight on the Scriptures* (Brooklyn: Watchtower Bible and Tract Society of New York, 1988), 1:853.

[12] It should be noted that, on the Christian view, the divine intellect *does* know all future events. If it were otherwise, God would not be omniscient, as entailed by his possession of all perfections.

just as it calls him God (John 20:28). It would seem reasonable to say that a mediator between two parties is generally not one of the parties, but he can still be (and usually is) of the same nature as each. So just because one man mediates between two others, it does not follow that he cannot have a human nature because they do. In fact, the Watchtower's own NWT reveals that Christ was "in God's form" but then "he emptied himself and took a slave's form and came to be in the likeness of men" (Phil. 2:6–7). So while most mediators can stand in the middle of two parties because they are not on either side, Christ, as mediator, perfectly stands in the middle between God and humans because he is on *both* sides in virtue of being fully God and fully man.

How could Jesus be God if he prayed to God? Was he praying to himself?

In the passages where Jesus prays to God, it is evident that he is speaking with the Father (Matt. 26:39 and John 11:41, for instance). Since Jesus is a person who is distinct from the Father, he is able to pray to the Father without praying to himself. If there were only one person in the Godhead and Jesus were praying to God, he would indeed be talking to himself—but this is not what the Bible says. This awkward and unorthodox position is held only by a few groups, such as Oneness Pentecostals, who deny that there are three Persons in the Godhead.

How could Jesus be God if the Father is greater than he (John 14:28)?

It is true that there are passages in Scripture where Jesus appears to be "less" than the Father. But again one must keep in mind what other passages say about Jesus' status and nature. As St. Paul says in Philippians 2:6–7, Jesus emptied himself, though he was "in the form of God." The Gospel of John (17:5) announces that this voluntary humiliation ceased with his glorification.

To understand this difference in status between Jesus on earth and the Father in heaven, one must understand what theologians call the "economy of salvation." In other words, the Father and the Son both have a role in bringing about the salvation of humans. It is quite clear from Scripture that Jesus' role involved an "emptying" of himself and his prerogatives as God. This is the very idea Paul promotes in Philippians 2:6–11, which is known as the *kenosis* hymn (from a Greek word meaning "to make empty"). So, in John 14:28, when Jesus says that the Father is "greater" than he, Jesus is speaking in reference to his position in the economy of salvation, to his freely chosen position as a "slave," and with regard to the fact that it was the Father who sent him.

Putting this concept in more modern terms, one person (a boss) can send another (an employee) on a task without being of a different nature than the one who is sent. A human can serve another human and still share the same human nature. In a like manner, Jesus does not lose his divine nature if he serves the Father.

How could Jesus be God if the Bible says that no one has seen God (John 1:18)?

What John means in John 1:18 is that no living person has seen what is called the Beatific Vision—the experience of God we will have in heaven. Also, John clarifies later in his Gospel that it is specifically God the Father that no one has seen (6:46). Man in his present state is not capable of gazing at the radiance of the face of God (Ex. 33:20), and so Jesus emptied himself of this glory for the sake of man at the Incarnation (Phil. 2:6–7).

Even God the Father is seen in various ways throughout the Old Testament (Gen. 12:7, 17:1, 28:13, 31:13), and one need not conclude from this (vis-à-vis John 1:18) that he is not God.

How could Jesus be God if Scripture says, "the head of every man is the Christ; in turn the head of a woman is the man; in turn the head of the Christ is God" (1 Cor. 11:3)?

If the husband is the head of the wife, does this mean that the wife must not have a human nature? Likewise, the fact that God the Father is the head of Christ does not mean that Christ cannot have a divine nature.

How could Jesus be God if he is wisdom Incarnate, since Proverbs 8:22–30 says that wisdom was created? "Jehovah himself produced me as [sic] *the beginning of his way, the earliest of his achievements long ago. . . . I came to be beside him as a master worker."*

Proverbs 8 nowhere says that wisdom was created. The Hebrew verb *qanah* which the NWT translates as "produced," would be better rendered as "possessed" or "acquired."

"But," the Watchtower reasons, "if wisdom was 'produced,' doesn't this mean that Jesus is not God?" In the literal sense of the text, the "production" of wisdom by God is a metaphor. If wisdom was created at a specific point in time, then there was a time when it was not. But was there ever a time that God was without wisdom? If there were, he would cease to be God, because one cannot lack wisdom and be omniscient at the same time. Thus, wisdom must have existed as long as God has existed—from eternity. When, in connection with the spiritual sense of the text, Jesus is seen as divine wisdom—the *Logos*—the "production" of wisdom would refer to the eternal procession of the Son from the Father.

How could Jesus be God if he is the only-begotten Son (John 3:16)?

Once again, it does not follow that Jesus was created because the term "only-begotten" (*monogenēs*) is applied to him. In Greek this word means "unique," or "unparalleled,"[13] or the only member of a particular kind. It does not necessarily mean "created" or "generated." In this case, it refers to the Son's eternal procession from the Father.

∼

Considering the above objections to Jesus' divinity, it is clear that the Watchtower would have its followers believe that Jehovah and Jesus are necessarily different beings, one being God Almighty and uncreated and the other being a "god" and created. The Bible tells another story. Below are verses that indicate that Jehovah's traits, powers, and titles are shared by Jesus. Since a mere creature,

---

[13] Kittel, 4:738.

no matter how exalted, cannot inherently possess divine attributes as well as the very character of God Almighty, the only way one can understand this sharing of traits is to acknowledge that Jesus must be God Almighty.

	JESUS	JEHOVAH
Mighty God	Is. 9:6	Is. 10:21
King of Kings	Rev. 19:13, 16	1 Tim. 6:15
Lord of Lords	Rev. 19:13, 16	1 Tim. 6:15
The only Savior	Acts 4:12	Is. 43:11
The First and the Last	Rev. 1:17	Is. 44:6
The Alpha and the Omega	Rev. 22:12–20	Rev. 1:8
Worshiped by angels	Heb. 1:6	Neh. 9:6
Unchanging	Heb. 13:8	Mal. 3:6
Created heaven and earth	Heb. 1:10	Neh. 9:6
Upholds the universe	Heb. 1:3	Neh. 9:6
From time indefinite	Mic. 5:2	Ps. 90:2
Redeems from iniquities	Titus 2:13–14	Ps. 130:7–8
Has power to forgive	Luke 5:20	Jer. 31:34
Wonderful Counselor	Is. 9:6	Is. 28:29
Lives in us	Gal. 2:20	2 Cor. 6:16
Omniscient	John 21:17	1 John 3:20
Gives eternal life	John 10:28	1 John 5:11
Judges the world	John 5:22	Ps. 96:13
To be worshiped	Rev. 5:13–14	Ps. 97:7
Calms the sea	Mark 4:41	Ps. 89:9
Will give to man according to his ways	Rev. 2:23	Jer. 17:10
To him every knee will bend and every tongue will confess he is Lord	Phil. 2:9–11	Is. 45:23

Perhaps one last point needs to be made with regard to the person of Christ. The Watchtower teaches that Jesus did not need to be God in order to redeem us, because Adam was a man and Christ was the second Adam. Jesus paid the ransom of one perfect human life—since that is what Adam lost—and that was all that was needed to reconcile man with God. This is not true. The fall of Adam affected, not just Adam, but the whole human race. Adam lost more than his own immortality. Further, because grave sins are offenses against an infinitely holy God, they incur an infinite debt. No human being, however perfect, is capable of paying an infinite debt. Thus God himself had to take the initiative to save us by paying the debt on our behalf. It is an appreciation of the gravity of our sins that points us to the necessity of the Redeemer's being God himself.

6

Is the Holy Spirit God?

Since the Trinity is unbiblical and false, the Holy Spirit surely is not God —or for that matter—even a person. It is merely God's impersonal active force, much like electricity, radio waves, or a radar beam.[1] Jehovah uses it to move believers to do his will.

Who—or what—is the Holy Spirit? This is one question that Watchtower adherents are not typically very well prepared to deal with. The Witnesses deny both the divinity and the personhood of the Holy Spirit, so each of these denials must be addressed separately, beginning with the latter.

In Acts 13:2 the Holy Spirit says, "Set Barnabas and Saul apart for *me* for the work to which *I* have called them"[2] (emphases added). In this verse, this "impersonal active force" reveals himself to be a person, since only a person can refer to himself as "I." Electricity, radio waves, or a radar beam cannot.[3] Scripture also states that the Holy Spirit can be lied to,[4] speak,[5] hear,[6] know the future,[7]

---

[1] *The Watchtower*, 15 July 1957, 432−35.

[2] See also Acts 10:19−20.

[3] This cannot be written off as a metaphor because it occurs, not in a symbolic book, like Revelation, but in the narrative of a nonsymbolic, historical book: Acts.

[4] Acts 5:3.

[5] Acts 8:29; 10:19, 20; 13:2.

[6] John 16:13−15.

[7] Acts 21:11.

know the "things of God,"[8] bear witness,[9] teach,[10] reprove,[11] pray and intercede,[12] love,[13] guide,[14] call,[15] be grieved,[16] consciously will,[17] feel hurt,[18] be outraged,[19] and be blasphemed.[20] Only a person has these attributes and abilities, and only God can be blasphemed.

That the Holy Spirit is a spirit does not mean that he cannot also be a person. After all, God is a spirit and Satan is a spirit, as are all angels, whether fallen or glorious—and all of these are persons.

Now one must show that he is God. Any number of biblical passages can be used for this. For example, Acts 5:1–4 explains that a lie to the Holy Spirit is a lie to God himself. The Bible contains a number of other passages where the Holy Spirit is on par with God the Father (Jehovah): Isaiah 44:24 insists that Jehovah alone is responsible for creation, and Malachi 2:10 states that there is but one creator. However, Job 33:4 and Psalm 104:30 explain that God's Spirit is the creator.

The Jews were said to have put Jehovah to the test in Exodus 17:2, but in the letter to the Hebrews (3:9) we see these words of God applied to the Holy Spirit, who notes that the Jews' ancestors "tested and tried me."

Jeremiah 31:33 reads, " 'For this is the covenant that I shall conclude with the house of Israel after those days,' is the utterance

---

[8] 1 Cor. 2:11.
[9] John 15:26.
[10] John 14:26.
[11] John 16:8–11.
[12] Rom. 8:26.
[13] Rom. 15:30.
[14] John 16:13.
[15] Acts 13:2.
[16] Eph. 4:30.
[17] 1 Cor. 12:11.
[18] Is. 63:10.
[19] Heb. 10:29.
[20] Mark 3:29.

of Jehovah. 'I will put my law within them, and in their heart I shall write it.' " In Hebrews 10:15–16, one reads, "Moreover the Holy Spirit also bears witness to us, for after it has said: 'This is the covenant that I shall covenant toward them after those days,' says Jehovah. 'I will put my laws in their hearts and in their minds I shall write them.' "

There is but one Lord (Eph. 4:5), yet both the Father and the Spirit claim they are he (Matt. 11:25 and 2 Cor. 3:17). In the NWT rendering of 2 Corinthians 3:17, Paul states explicitly, "Jehovah is the Spirit."

The Holy Spirit is everlasting (Heb. 9:14), all-knowing (1 Cor. 2:10), and omnipresent (Ps. 139:7), but these are attributes that only God has.

In view of these considerations, the only logical conclusion one can draw is that the Holy Spirit is God.

7

Is God's Name Jehovah?

"Jehovah" is God's name, and "everyone who calls on the name of Jehovah will be saved" (Rom. 10:13). Many scholars favor the spelling Yahweh, *but it is uncertain and there is no agreement among them. On the other hand,* Jehovah *is the form of the name that is most readily recognized, because it has been used in English for centuries. In the New Testament, uses of the word* Kurios, *when referring to the Father, should be rendered "Jehovah."*[1]

In considering these statements, it is instructive to look at the Watchtower Bible dictionary, *Aid to Bible Understanding*:

The first recorded use of this form [Jehovah] dates from the 13th century C.E. Raymundus Martini, a Spanish monk of the Dominican Order, used it in his book *Pugeo Fidei* of the year 1270. Hebrew scholars generally favor "Yahweh" as the most likely pronunciation.[2]

Interestingly, these facts were omitted from the most recent Watchtower Bible dictionary, *Insight on the Scriptures*. This omission, however, does not change the fact that even the Watchtower affirmed that the term *Jehovah* is—of all things—a *Catholic* coinage from the Middle Ages! Moreover, numerous reference works, such as the *Jewish Encyclopedia, Encyclopedia Judaica, Webster's Encyclopedia, Encyclopedia Britannica, Universal Jewish Encyclopedia, Encyclopedia Americana, Encyclopedia International, The Inter-*

---

[1] *Reasoning from the Scriptures* (Brooklyn: Watchtower Bible and Tract Society of New York, 1985), 191–99.

[2] *Aid to Bible Understanding* (Brooklyn: Watchtower Bible and Tract Society of New York, 1971), 884–85.

preter's Dictionary of the Bible, and *The New Schaff-Herzog Encyclopedia*, agree that the rendering "Jehovah" is erroneous and was never used by the Jews. So where does the name Jehovah come from? James Akin explains:

> When the word LORD appears in Scripture, it will be in the Old Testament and is translating the Hebrew word for the name of God—YHWH, or JHVH (biblical Hebrew has no vowels, only consonants). Any vowels later added are not a part of the original text. The Ten Commandments forbid anyone to misuse the name of Yahweh, stating: "You shall not misuse the name of Yahweh your God, for Yahweh will not hold anyone who misuses his name guiltless" (Ex. 20:7; cf. Deut. 5:11).
>
> Although the name Yahweh was used freely in the early history of Israel, by the time of Jesus the Jews (especially the Pharisees) had become scrupulous about breaking the Mosaic Law and, in an attempt to "build a wall" around the commandments of the Law so that no one could even get close to breaking them, they ruled that no one should speak the name of Yahweh—ever. The only exception to this was during one feast day of the year when the priest would intone the actual name "Yahweh" once during the liturgy.
>
> This prohibition on saying "Yahweh" created a problem for people reading the Bible out loud in synagogue liturgies. Since the name of Yahweh was freely used in the Scripture texts, what were they to say in its place as they read the Bible out loud? The answer that was reached was that they were to say the word "Adonai" instead. Adonai is the Hebrew word for "lord," or actually "my lord."
>
> When the Septuagint (the Greek version of the Old Testament) was translated, it replaced the Hebrew word YHWH with the Greek word for "lord" (*kurios*).
>
> [W]hen vowels were eventually introduced into the Jewish alphabet, they came in the form of vowel points above and below the consonant letters that were written on the page of Scripture. Because the custom of saying "Adonai" instead of "Yahweh" was already in place, when the Jews added vowel points to the Old Testament, they used the vowel points for "Adonai" (a-o-a) whenever they encountered the word "YHWH," giving us "Yahowah," which is transliterated into English as "Jehovah." Thus the Jeho-

vah's Witnesses, for all their insistence on the divine name, have actually named themselves after something that isn't the name of God. Jehovah is not God's true name. Based on the patristic and other evidence available, the actual way the divine name was pronounced was "Yahweh," not "Jehovah."

Furthermore, because they have named themselves after something that isn't God's name and then gone out and rubbed this in the face of the world, they have actually perpetuated the "hiding" of the divine name by reinforcing in the world's memory the name Jehovah instead of Yahweh.[3]

Reading New Testament Greek, one quickly notices a problem for the Witnesses that the Watchtower has never been able to explain fully. The authors of the New Testament never use the word *Jehovah*, or even *Yahweh*. Even in quotes from the Old Testament where the divine name had been used, the authors of the New Testament decided to use the word *Lord* (Greek, *kurios*) instead. The Watchtower explains that the original manuscripts surely must have had *Jehovah* in them, but later copyists from the "apostate" Church altered them to hide the true name of God.[4] To correct this, the NWT added the word *Jehovah* 237 times in the New Testament.[5] In the appendix to the NWT the reader is assured:

> To avoid overstepping the bounds of a translator into the field of exegesis, we have been most cautious about rendering the divine name in the Christian Greek Scriptures, always carefully considering the Hebrew Scriptures as a background. We have looked for agreement from available Hebrew versions of the Christian Greek Scriptures to confirm our rendering.[6]

---

[3] From the question on " 'LORD' & 'Lord' " in "The Internet Question Box" at *www.jamesakin.com*.

[4] *Aid to Bible Understanding*, 887; "The Divine Name That Will Endure Forever" (Brooklyn: Watchtower Bible and Tract Society of New York, 1984), 25.

[5] Ibid., 888.

[6] *New World Translation*, 1640 (appendix 1).

However, the Watchtower doesn't mention here that there is no early manuscript evidence to support such a change, since it was not until the fourteenth century that a Jewish translator named Shem Tob ben Shaprut used the divine name in his Hebrew translation of Matthew.[7] Even then, he would not have used the term *Jehovah*, but the Tetragrammaton (YHWH).

Did the original authors of the New Testament use the name Jehovah before apostates altered the text to hide the name of God? There is absolutely no trace of that name's being used in the oldest manuscripts. There are thousands of ancient manuscripts of the Bible in Greek, Hebrew, Syriac, Coptic, Georgian, Ethiopian, Arabic, Gothic, Armenian, and Latin—but not one of them uses the Tetragrammaton (YHWH) in the New Testament, let alone Jehovah.

Beyond the manuscript evidence, the witness of the early Christians is also unanimous. Christians often suffered martyrdom for the faith, and they were scrupulous about preserving the accuracy of every word of Scripture. Take for example, the people of Oea. St. Augustine wrote to St. Jerome:

> We have come to this that a brother Bishop (of Oea), having ordered your translation to be read in the church to which he was accredited, people were disturbed because you had rendered a passage from the prophet Jonas in a very different manner from that which had grown old in all their memories and which so many generations had repeated. All the people were in an uproar; the Greeks especially, passionately accusing you of having falsified the text. . . . Our Bishop found himself obliged to rectify the passage as being erroneous in order to retain his people who were on the verge of abandoning him.[8]

If the people of Oea were infuriated over a translation of one passage from a minor prophet in the Old Testament, is it plausible that the very name of God was torn out of the New Testament 237 times by apostates, and not one Christian complained?

---

[7] *Aid to Bible Understanding*, 887.

[8] Augustine, *Letters* 71:5.

The reason the authors of the New Testament never used the word *Jehovah* is that they had never heard of that mispronunciation. The word *Yahweh* was never used in the New Testament because they were following the custom of their day, reverencing the name by refraining from saying it. Different ages show reverence in different ways. It is the reverence itself, not how it is shown, that is central.

8

Did Jesus Die on a
Torture Stake or a Cross?

Watchtower publications show Jesus on an upright stake instead of on a traditional cross because stauros in classical Greek meant merely an upright stake, or pale. The cross is an ancient pagan sign, a Tau, for the Babylonian god Tammuz. It was adopted by Christendom after the great apostasy in order to curry favor with the pagans.[1]

The Watchtower's use of the phrase "classical Greek" will sound scholarly to the unsuspecting reader, who will assume that the Watchtower has again provided him with the ancient truths of the Bible that apostate Christendom has lost. But one significant fact is omitted here: The New Testament was not written in classical Greek, the form of Greek spoken between 1000 and 330 B.C., so it does not matter what *stauros* meant in that dialect. The manuscripts of the New Testament are in *Koine* Greek—which is Hellenistic rather than classical Greek—in which *stauros* can be translated as (1) an upright stake with a cross-beam above it, (2) two intersecting beams of equal length, or (3) a vertical, pointed stake.[2]

During an execution in which a *stauros* was used, the condemned criminal would carry a crossbeam (known in Latin as the *patibulum*) to the place where the stake (*stipes*) had already been erected.

---

[1] *Reasoning from the Scriptures* (Brooklyn: Watchtower Tract and Bible Society of New York, 1985), 89–93.

[2] Gerhard Kittel and Gerhard Friedrich, eds. *Theological Dictionary of the New Testament* (Grand Rapids: Eerdmans, 1971), 7:572.

He was then tied or nailed to the beam he had carried, which was placed atop the erect pale.[3] The executioners would not have had the criminal carry the beam to the place of execution, only to take it from him, dig a hole for it, and mount him upon it. The vertical stake would already have been planted for the *patibulum* to be hung upon it. So the Watchtower is right in saying that Jesus was killed on a stake but wrong in denying that there was a crossbeam to which he was nailed and which hung atop this stake. If the New Testament authors wished to convey that Christ died on a torture stake, it is likely that they would have used the Greek word *skolops*. However, the Biblical writers never use this word to describe the instrument of Christ's death.

Aside from the Greek evidence, the New Testament provides further support for the Crucifixion. For example, if Jesus was impaled through both palms with *one* nail—as Watchtower literature depicts[4]—Scripture would not say that he had prints of the *nails* in his hands (John 20:25). If the Lord had been executed on a "torture stake" (this is how the NWT renders the word *stauros*), the Roman soldiers would not have used two nails to pierce his hands. Two nails would only be necessary if his arms were outstretched on a crossbeam.

Watchtower literature states that the symbol of the cross comes from *Tau*, the initial letter of the name Tammuz, a Babylonian god. Such misinformation originated in Alexander Hislop's highly inaccurate book *The Two Babylons*, from which the Watchtower freely quotes.[5] But is the *Tau* simply a pagan sign? If so, God himself commands that a pagan mark (*Tau*) be placed on the foreheads of the righteous in Ezekiel 9:4, 6—eight verses after Tammuz worship is repudiated (Ez. 8:14)! In fact, early Christian writers such as Tertullian and Origen considered this to be a prefigurement

---

[3] Ibid., 573.

[4] *You Can Live Forever in Paradise on Earth* (Brooklyn: Watchtower Bible and Tract Society of New York, 1982), 170.

[5] For a non-Catholic refutation of Hislop's claims, read Ralph Woodrow's *The Babylon Connection?* (Riverside, California: Ralph Woodrow Evangelistic Association, 1997).

of the cross of Christ.[6] If Jehovah has no qualms about using a crosslike symbol, the Jehovah's Witnesses should not, either.

Are there pagan symbols that predate Christianity and resemble the cross? Yes, just as there are countless references in paganism to obelisks and other objects that look like a "torture stake." The symbol of two intersecting lines can certainly be found in ancient cultures, as can straight lines, curves, triangles, crescents, squares, and any other shape imaginable. The fact that some pagan cultures used a crosslike symbol certainly in no way precluded the use of a crossbeam in the Roman executions in first century Palestine —nor does it mean that the shape of the cross was used in pagan worship or, especially, that the cross was forced upon Christian worship despite the facts of Christ's death.

Early Christians did not adopt the cross as a pagan worship symbol that they were enthused by and wanted to use in pagan worship. The early Christians used the symbol of the cross for the simple reason that Christ died on one. Moreover, the use of the sign of the cross is clearly attested in ancient sources. As Tertullian, for example, remarked in the second century: "In all our travels, in our coming in and going out, in putting on our clothes and our shoes, at table, in going to rest, whatever employment occupies us, we mark our forehead with the sign of the cross."[7] He even mentions this among other practices of apostolic origin. In contrast, there is no historical evidence of Christians marking themselves with the sign of the "torture stake."

Another important consideration is that no one has discovered any ancient Christian art depicting Christ on a stake. If anything, all the evidence points to a cruciform shape. One early depiction of Christ's death, known as the Palatine crucifix, dates from the second century during the reign of the Roman emperor Septimius Severus (A.D. 198–211).[8] Over a century ago, Roman archaeol-

---

[6] Tertullian, *Against Marcion* 3:22. For an even earlier Christian witness to the *Tau* as a prefiguration of the cross, see the *Letter of Barnabas* 9.

[7] *The Chaplet (De Corona)* 3.

[8] Orazio Marucchi, *Manual of Christian Archaeology* (Paterson, New Jersey: St. Anthony Guild Press, 1935), 44.

ogists discovered this ancient graffito scratched into a wall on the Palatine Hill in Rome. The carving depicts a boy reverencing his God, who is crucified *with arms outstretched and nailed to a crossbeam*. (The caption scrawled beneath the crucifix reads, "Alexamenos adores his God.") The crucified God is given the head of a jack-ass, since the purpose of the depiction was to mock Alexamenos's Christian faith.

Additional archaeological evidence to support Christ's death on a cross includes an example from the latter part of the first century. Recently unearthed in the city of Herculaneum is a

> primitive Christian oratory in the upper room of the so-called "House of Bicentenary" at Herculaneum. A whitish stuccoed panel shows the imprint of a large cross, probably metallic, that had been removed. . . . Before it are the remains of a small wooden altar, charred by lava from the eruption of Mt. Vesuvius in 79 A.D.[9]

Because of the date of the volcanic eruption, the image of the cross must have been painted within fifty years of the Crucifixion. Again, it is unreasonable to think that the shape of the instrument of Christ's death was forgotten or misrepresented so soon after the Crucifixion.

Consider yet another factor. Only thirty years after the death of Christ, St. Peter was also crucified. This event was spoken of in the second century by Tertullian, and again by Origen: "Peter was crucified at Rome with his head downwards, as he himself had desired to suffer."[10] Tertullian adds:

> If you are near Italy, you have Rome, where authority is ever within reach. How fortunate is this Church for which the apostles have poured out their whole teaching with their blood, where Peter has emulated the Passion of the Lord, where Paul was crowned with the death of John [the Baptist].[11]

In another work he again mentions Peter's crucifixion: "The budding faith Nero first made bloody in Rome. There Peter was

---

[9] Paul Maier, *First Christians: Pentecost and the Spread of Christianity* (New York: Harper and Row, 1976), 141.

[10] Eusebius, *Ecclesiastical History* 2:i.

[11] *The Prescription against Heretics* 35.

girded by another, since he was bound to the cross."[12] Clearly these examples confirm that a cross, not a torture stake, was used as the instrument of Christ's death.[13]

Saints Irenaeus and Justin Martyr (both recognized by the Watchtower as "leading religious teachers in the early centuries after Christ's birth"[14]) confirm that Jesus did not die on a torture stake. Irenaeus said, "The very form of the cross, too, has five extremities, two in length, two in breadth, and one in the middle, on which [last] the person rests who is fixed by the nails."[15]

After speaking of how Moses' outstretched arms were a prefiguring of the cross of Christ,[16] Justin Martyr explains how the cross was erected: "For the one beam is placed upright . . . [and] the other beam is fitted on to it."[17] Both of these patristic writings date within approximately a century of the life of St. John the apostle, and Irenaeus was taught by Polycarp, a disciple of John. Once again, the cross and not the upright stake is clearly attested to in these writings. On the other hand, the Watchtower has been unable to furnish any early Christian evidence that Jesus was put to death on a pale, or upright stake.

Evidence for the Crucifixion has continued to grow, as can be seen in recent discoveries. In 1968, the remains of a crucified man from A.D. 70 were found in a burial cave at Giv'at ha-Mivtar in Jerusalem. The findings of the archaeologists were released in the report "Anthropological Observations on the Skeletal Remains from Giv'at ha-Mivtar," published in the *Israel Exploration Journal* and written by N. Haas of the department of anatomy at Hebrew University. After investigating the remains of the man executed

---

[12] *Antidote for the Scorpion's Sting* 15.

[13] Witnesses cannot respond that the word *stauros* is being mistranslated as "cross," since Tertullian's surviving writings are not in Greek but Latin, from which we get the words *cross* (*crux*) and *crucify* (*crucifigere*).

[14] *Should You Believe in the Trinity?* (Brooklyn: Watchtower Bible and Tract Society of New York, 1989), 7.

[15] *Against Heresies* 2:4:24.

[16] *Dialogue with Trypho the Jew* 90.

[17] Ibid., 91.

under Roman rule (as Christ was), he explained that "the upper
limbs were stretched out, each stabbed by a nail in the forearm."[18]
In harmony with such findings, earlier Watchtower literature repeatedly depicted Christ crucified or Christ carrying his cross,[19]
affirming as a fact that "Jesus was crucified upon the cross."[20]

Ironically, beside Charles Taze Russell's tombstone is a massive
pyramid emblazoned with a cross-and-crown symbol. In 1928,
the Watchtower announced that this "Cross and Crown" symbol,
which had been used for years on the cover of *Zion's Watch Tower*
and *The Watch Tower*, "to Brother Rutherford's mind was Baby-
lonish and should be discontinued."[21] So, the image of the cross
was officially dropped from Watchtower publications in 1931.[22]

Witnesses often object to the practice of wearing a cross as a
necklace or as any form of adornment. To the mind of a Witness,
it would be like wearing a miniature electric chair around your
neck after your friend had died in one. Yet, Christians do not
glory in the cross because of what it did to Jesus but because of
what Jesus did through it! Paul knew that this would be a stumbling block to some, foolishness to others (1 Cor. 1:23), but it
is the very power of God (1 Cor. 1:18). For this reason, he said,
"For I resolved to know nothing while I was with you except
Jesus Christ, and him crucified" (1 Cor. 2:2; NAB).

---

[18] Clayton F. Bower, "Cross or Torture Stake?" *This Rock* (October 1991),
9.

[19] *The Photo Drama of Creation* (Brooklyn: International Bible Students Asso-
ciation, 1914), 12, 69, 88; J. F. Rutherford, *The Harp of God* (Brooklyn: Watch
Tower Bible and Tract Society, 1928), 113; J. F. Rutherford, *Life* (Brooklyn:
Watch Tower Bible and Tract Society, 1929), 198.

[20] *Life*, 216.

[21] *1975 Yearbook of Jehovah's Witnesses* (Brooklyn: Watchtower Bible and
Tract Society of New York, 1974), 148.

[22] Ibid.

9

Did Christ's Body Rise?

It was necessary that the man Christ Jesus should die but just as necessary that the man Christ Jesus should never live again, should remain dead, should remain our ransom-price to all eternity. After all, if Jesus took up his body again, he would not be giving up his life as a ransom.[1] Thus the man Jesus is dead—forever.[2] We deny that He was raised in the flesh, and challenge any statement to that effect as being unscriptural.[3] Jesus' fleshly body was disposed of by Jehovah God—dissolved into its constitutive elements or atoms,[4] or perhaps it was dissolved into gas or preserved somewhere as a memorial to God's love, perhaps to be exhibited to the people of the millennial age.[5] After he rose, he used a body with wound holes in order to convince Thomas of who he was.[6] Only because Thomas would not believe did Jesus appear in a body like that in which he had died.[7] He was recreated by Jehovah God as an invisible spirit creature.[8] The Bible agrees that he was "put to death in the flesh, but . . . made alive in the spirit" (1 Pet.

---

[1] *You Can Live Forever in Paradise on Earth* (Brooklyn: Watchtower Bible and Tract Society of New York, 1982), 143.

[2] Charles Taze Russell, *Studies in the Scriptures* (Brooklyn: International Bible Students Association, 1899), 5:454.

[3] Charles Taze Russell, *Studies in the Scriptures* (Brooklyn: People's Pulpit Association, 1917), 7:57.

[4] *The Watchtower*, 1 September 1953, 518.

[5] Charles Taze Russell, *Studies in the Scriptures* (Brooklyn: International Bible Students Association, 1889), 2:129; and J. F. Rutherford, *The Harp of God* (Brooklyn: Watch Tower Bible and Tract Society of New York, 1928), 172–73.

[6] *You Can Live Forever*, 145.

[7] *From Paradise Lost to Paradise Regained* (Brooklyn: Watchtower Bible and Tract Society of New York, 1958), 144.

[8] *Reasoning from the Scriptures* (Brooklyn: Watchtower Bible and Tract Society of New York, 1985), 217–18.

3:18). The Scriptures do not reveal what became of that body, except that it did not decay or corrupt (Acts 2:27–31).

Few teachings of the Watchtower are hidden from the prospective convert as much as this one. Some Witnesses are even unaware that the Watchtower actually teaches this. It is understandable that it is not given much attention, since Scripture testifies so clearly against it.

While Jesus was passing through the temple in Jerusalem, some Jewish people asked him for a sign. He replied, "Break down this temple, and in three days I will raise it up" (John 2:19). They understood him to be speaking of the temple building, but John clarifies that Jesus had something else in mind: "He was talking about the temple of *his body*" (John 2:21; emphasis added). The Greek here is *sōmatos autou*, "the body of himself." Jesus unequivocally teaches that he will raise up his body after three days. There is no suggestion—as the Witnesses maintain—that the ransom he paid for the sin of the world would be revoked if his body were to rise again. It was the raising of his body that conquered death and completed the redemption of mankind. If all that was needed to redeem man was the sacrifice of the body of Christ, the Resurrection was superfluous.

After he had risen, Jesus showed that his promise had been fulfilled, "See my hands and my feet, that it is I myself; feel me and see, because a *spirit does not have flesh and bones just as you behold that I have.* . . . Do you have something there to eat?" (Luke 24:39, 41; emphasis added). Jesus also insisted that Thomas place his finger into his wounded side, to prove that he had indeed risen from the dead (John 20:27). But why would Jesus offer a body to prove that his spirit had risen? In Matthew 28:6, why would the angel offer the empty tomb as proof that Jesus rose if his body is forever dead?

Jehovah's Witnesses argue that since "flesh and blood cannot inherit God's kingdom" (1 Cor. 15:50), Jesus could not have been resurrected in the flesh. What does Paul have in mind, though? In 1 Corinthians 15, St. Paul is speaking about the resurrection of the dead and explaining that mortal and corruptible bodies will not enter heaven. He is not denying the resurrection of the body, for he goes on to explain that the mortal and corruptible bodies will "put on immortality." Far from proposing that the mortal bodies will be cast off, he says that "we shall all be changed" into sinless, incorruptible, and immortal beings:

> For this which is corruptible must *put on* incorruption, and this which is mortal must *put on* immortality. But when [this which is corruptible *puts on* incorruption] this which is mortal *puts on* immortality, then the saying will take place that is written: "Death is swallowed up forever." "Death, where is your victory? Death, where is your sting?" The sting producing death is sin. . . . But thanks to God, for he gives us the victory through our Lord Jesus Christ! (1 Cor 15:53–57; brackets in original, emphases added)

Because Christ's body rose, death was conquered and "the Lord Jesus Christ . . . will refashion our humiliated body to be conformed to his glorious body" (Phil. 3:21). Paul reiterates this when he declares that "he that raised up Christ Jesus from the dead will also make YOUR mortal bodies alive through his spirit that resides in you" (Rom. 8:11).

Witnesses also call attention to 1 Corinthians 15:45, which explains that Christ has become "a life-giving spirit," and conclude from this that he could not have a glorified human body. While there are purely spiritual beings that have no bodies (e.g., angels), it does not follow that Jesus was one of them, since the resurrected Christ emphasized to the disciples that "a spirit does not have flesh and bones just as you behold that I have" (Luke 24:39). So, Jesus does have a glorified body that is not mere spirit. If it were mere spirit, it could not be called a body. That would be a contradiction in terms. Rather, he has a glorified body with spiritual powers.

Certain details in the Gospels' Resurrection accounts are seized upon by the Watchtower to promote the idea that Jesus was merely a spirit. For example, they argue that Jesus was unrecognizable after the Resurrection, because his spirit assumed various bodies. However, in the one instance in which the disciples failed to recognize Jesus, the Bible explains that "their eyes were kept from recognizing him" (Luke 24:15–16). Scripture is clear that the disciples were supernaturally *prevented* from recognizing Jesus, not that there was something inherently unrecognizable about Jesus' body.

Witnesses also argue that he must have been a spirit if he was able to pass through a door to enter the upper room (John 20:26). First, the text does not say that he passed through the doors, merely that he "came, although the doors were locked."[9] Second, a glorified human body does not have the same limitations as a nonglorified body. And third, if Enoch and Elijah could be taken up into heaven bodily (Gen. 5:24; 2 Kgs. 2:1–13; Heb. 11:5), Jesus could surely appear in a room without needing to open a door. If Jesus was able to defy the laws of nature by walking on water in a mortal body (Mark 6:48), the glorified body of Christ should surely have still further abilities.

There is no question that Jesus' body had truly risen from the dead. No Christian was under the impression that he was invisibly raised as Michael the archangel while God the Father supposedly dissolved his natural body into atoms—as the Watchtower has claimed. Can you imagine Mary Magdalene running to the apostles across the hills of Jerusalem, tears of joy streaming down her cheeks, thrilled with the good news that Jehovah God had dissolved Jesus into constitutive elements and raised him as an invisible spirit creature, Michael? For the Witnesses' own spiritual

---

[9] There are ways in which it would be possible for a physical body to arrive on the other side of a wall without having to move through the intervening space. Mathematician Edwin Abbott, in his short, allegorical novel *Flatland: A Romance in Many Dimensions* (reprint, Mineola, New York: Dover, 1992), explains a number of ways in which adding a dimension allows things to be accomplished by physical bodies that otherwise would be impossible. If we adapt one of his examples, Jesus could have been on one side of a locked door and from there shifted himself to heaven. Then, from heaven, he could have shifted himself back to earth on the other side of the door. Thus he could come to the disciples even though the door was locked, without having to physically move *through* the door.

good, the joy of the bodily risen Christ must be brought to them, for "if Christ has not been raised, your faith is vain; you are still in your sins" (1 Cor. 15:17; NAB).

Did Christ Already Return?

The year 1914 marked the end of the "Gentile Times" our Lord mentioned in Luke 21:24, as well as the time for Christ's foretold presence.[1] Since Jesus returned invisibly in 1914, he will have no visible Second Coming. Some wrongfully expect a literal fulfillment of the symbolic statements of the Bible. Since no earthly men have ever seen the Father, neither will they see the glorified Son.[2] Just as Jesus went away (quietly, secretly, so far as the world was concerned, and unbeknownst except to his followers), in this manner, he comes again.[3] He did not rise physically, so he will not return physically. The Greek word for coming (parousia) is better translated as "presence." So, he is already present, and not yet to come.

Following Russell's chronology, the Watchtower used to teach that the Bible proved that the second "presence" of Jesus began in A.D. 1874.[4] Russell had also predicted that Armageddon would come in 1874, but he revised this date to 1914, then 1915, and finally 1918. By the time 1918 rolled around, he had passed away, so no later dates were set. Now the Watchtower has settled on 1914 as the date that Christ came back to earth—invisibly.

Of all these peculiar teachings regarding Christ's return, one first has to ask, "Why 1914?" How the Watchtower chose 1914 is not a simple matter to explain, but this, in brief, is the chronol-

---

[1] *The Watchtower*, 1 April 1986, 31.

[2] *Let God Be True* (Brooklyn: Watchtower Bible and Tract Society of New York, 1946), 186.

[3] Charles Taze Russell, *Studies in the Scriptures* (Brooklyn: International Bible Students Association, 1889), 2:154.

[4] *Prophecy* (Brooklyn: Watchtower Bible and Tract Society of New York, 1929), 65.

ogy: Satan's kingdom is supposed to have begun in 607 B.C., when Babylon overcame Jerusalem. At this time, the world was handed over to Satan for 2,520 years. Why the span of 2,520 years? The Watchtower explains, "The duration of a year as so used is indicated to be 360 days, inasmuch as three and a half times are shown to equal 'a thousand two hundred and sixty days' at Revelation 12:6, 14. 'Seven times' [from Dan. 4:10–17], according to this count, would equal 2520 days."[5] But 2,520 years after 607 B.C. is A.D. 1914, so this marks the end of what is called the "Gentile Times," when Jesus/Michael cast Satan out of heaven and began his invisible reign.

There are several problems with this elaborate plan, and the most notable is that the date 607 B.C. as the downfall of Jerusalem is wrong. This downfall at the hands of the Babylonians is accepted by scholars as having occurred in 587 B.C., throwing the Watchtower's entire chronology off by twenty years. In fact, Ray Franz, a former Governing Body member and now an ex-Witness, discovered this truth for himself while researching an article on chronology he was writing for the Watchtower's *Aid to Bible Understanding* book:

> Months of research were spent on this one subject of "Chronology" and it resulted in the longest article in the *Aid* publication. Much of the time was spent endeavoring to find some proof, some backing in history, for the 607 B.C.E. date so crucial to our calculations for 1914. . . . We found absolutely nothing in support of 607 B.C.E. All historians pointed to a date twenty years later. . . . Everything pointed to a period twenty years shorter than our published chronology claimed.[6]

Moving beyond the question of chronology, what does Scripture have to say on the topic of the Second Coming? First, Jesus himself states quite plainly that no one will be able to predict it

---

[5] *Aid to Bible Understanding* (Brooklyn: Watchtower Bible and Tract Society of New York, 1971), 96.

[6] Ray Franz, *Crisis of Conscience* (Atlanta: Commentary Press, 1992), 25–26.

(Matt. 24:36–44), which alone proves the Watchtower's efforts at setting dates misguided. Second, is it an event or a "presence" that one might miss if he isn't paying attention? The Greek word that is often translated as "coming" (*parousia*) can indeed be translated as "presence," but the New Testament is very clear that this presence will be a visible one:

> *[A]ll the tribes of the earth* will beat themselves in lamentation, and *they will see the Son of man coming* on the clouds of heaven with power and great glory. (Matt. 24:30; emphases added)

> Look! He is coming with the clouds, and *every eye will see him.* (Rev. 1:7; emphasis added)

> *[Y]ou will see the Son of man* sitting at the right hand of power and coming on the clouds of heaven. (Matt. 26:64; emphasis added)

> [A]nd the second time that he *appears.* (Heb. 9:28; emphasis added)

Paul does not expect an invisible and quiet Second Coming when he calls on others to "wait for the happy hope, *and glorious manifestation* of the great God and of [the] Savior of us, Christ Jesus" (Titus 2:13; emphasis added). Jesus came visibly the first time, and the Second Coming will be likewise. Also, the disciples were informed by an angel that, just as Jesus ascended visibly and gloriously, he "will come thus in the same manner as YOU have beheld him going into the sky" (Acts 1:11, cf. 1:9). The angel would not have asked the apostles why they were looking into the sky if Jesus' ascension was invisible, so it was visible; thus, that is the manner in which he will return. In Matthew 24:23–27, we are advised that

> if anyone says to YOU, "Look! Here is the Christ," or "There!" do not believe it. For false Christs and false prophets will arise. . . . For just as the lightning comes out of eastern parts and shines over to western parts, so the presence [Greek, *parousia*, "coming"] of the Son of man will be.

Regrettably, this warning by Jesus applies to the Watchtower. Russell had taught that Jesus returned in 1874. He declared, in essence, "Look! The invisible Christ is here." But Jesus said no one would miss his Second Advent, as it would be like lightning flashing across the world.

Another difficulty for the idea of a 1914 return can be found in 1 Corinthians 11:26, which reads, "For as often as YOU eat this loaf and drink this cup, YOU keep proclaiming the death of the Lord, *until* he arrives" (emphasis added). If he arrived in 1914 as the Watchtower asserts, then why is the Memorial of the Lord (their version of a Holy Thursday celebration) celebrated each year? Their own worship practice contradicts their theology.

11

Who Goes to Heaven?

God has revealed that in the end there will be an earthly class and a heavenly class of believers. Only the anointed 144,000 of Revelation 7 and 14 will enter heaven, while the remainder who are not annihilated will live forever as a great crowd on earth in paradise. They will exist in peace as in the Garden of Eden, without aches, pains, disease, famine, violence, wrinkled skin, or gray hair.[1] This is the plan God had intended for man before the fall, and he will restore this ideal state. Psalm 37 clearly teaches that the 'evildoers themselves will be cut off, but those hoping in Jehovah are the ones that will possess the earth. . . . The righteous themselves will possess the earth, and they will reside forever upon it." Jesus reiterates this in his Sermon on the Mount, promising some that they will "inherit the earth." (Matt. 5:5)

Revelation 7 and 14 are the two passages most commonly used by the Watchtower to support its idea that heaven's total occupancy will be 144,000. Here is what the passages say:

I saw four angels standing upon the four corners of the earth . . . and I saw another angel . . . saying: "Do not harm the earth or the sea or the trees until we have sealed the slaves of our God on their foreheads." And I heard the number of those that were sealed, a hundred and forty-four thousand, sealed out of every tribe of the sons of Israel: Out of the tribe of Judah twelve thousand sealed; out of the tribe of Reuben twelve thousand. . . . After these things I saw, and, look! a great crowd, which no man was able to number, out of all nations and tribes and peoples and tongues, standing before the throne and before the Lamb. (Rev. 7:1–9)

---

[1] *Let God Be True* (Brooklyn: Watchtower Bible and Tract Society of New York, 1952), 267–68.

And I saw, and, look! the Lamb standing upon the Mount Zion, and with him a hundred and forty-four thousand having his name and the name of his Father written on their foreheads . . . the hundred and forty four thousand who had been bought from the earth. These are the ones that did not defile themselves with women; in fact, they are virgins . . . and no falsehood was found in their mouths. (Rev. 14:1–5)

What the Bible says here is not compatible with the Watchtower understanding of these passages: If Revelation 7 and 14 are to be taken literally, there would be 144,000 Jewish male virgins that were taken from a square-shaped earth and are now worshiping a lamb in heaven. This would mean that St. Peter (not a virgin), the Blessed Virgin Mary (not a male), and Charles Taze Russell (not a Jew) could not be in heaven. Reading one verse literally while taking the rest of the chapter symbolically—in this particular case the very next verses—is dangerous and faulty exegesis.

Like the rest of the details given about the group, the number 144,000 should not be taken literally. The number 144,000 is the square of twelve (the number of the tribes of Israel), multiplied by a thousand, which is symbolic of the New Israel, the Church. The Witnesses retort that the number 144,000 cannot be symbolic, since a "great crowd" is mentioned afterward. From this, they conclude that "if the number 144,000 were not literal it would lack meaning as a contrast to the 'great crowd.' "[2]

At this point, their argument turns against itself. Revelation 7 describes the 144,000 coming from the twelve tribes of Israel, and the great crowd as being from "all nations and tribes and peoples and tongues." So if the number 144,000 must be literal to preserve the contrast from the great crowd, the twelve tribes must also be literal for the same reason. Thus, Witnesses who think they have "heavenly hope" must be from one of the twelve tribes mentioned in Revelation 7:5–8.

Beyond this, in Revelation 14, the 144,000 stand before the

---

[2] *Reasoning from the Scriptures* (Brooklyn: Watchtower Tract and Bible Society of New York, 1985), 167.

twenty-four elders mentioned in Revelation 4:4, bringing the total to at least 144,024 people. But there are still more to come.
Revelation 7:9 speaks of a countless multitude before the throne,
which is in heaven (Rev. 14:1–3). Witnesses counter that "before the throne" does not mean in heaven, but, rather, standing
before the throne while on earth, seeing Jehovah with "eyes of
faith." Being before the throne is considered "an approved condition." But Scripture could not be clearer: The "great crowd"
is "in heaven" (Rev. 19:1), "in his temple" (7:15).

At first, Charles Taze Russell taught that the great crowd mentioned in Revelation 7 was a secondary heavenly class that would
be saved to heaven out of the tribulation.[3] This teaching was later
confirmed in a Watchtower publication, which noted that the great
crowd of Revelation 7:9 would be in heaven and not on earth.[4]
This original interpretation was held for several decades and then
jettisoned in favor of the current interpretation. Under the leadership of Joseph Rutherford, the Watchtower held a conference
in 1935 and decided authoritatively that the 144,000 would end
up in heaven, while the rest of the saved would remain on earth.[5]
The "two-class" system became official teaching.

The Bible does speak of there being two classes—the saved and
the damned. In the book of Revelation (21:27), one reads that all
those with their names in the book of life are in heaven, while all
whose names are not in the book of life are thrown into the "lake
of fire and sulphur, where . . . they will be tormented day and
night, forever and ever. . . . Furthermore, whoever was not found
written in the book of life was hurled into the lake of fire" (20:10,
15). In seeing the holy city New Jerusalem (heaven), John notes
that "anything not sacred and anyone that carries on a disgusting
thing and a lie will in no way enter into it; only those written in

---

[3] *Watchtower Reprints*, 458 (*Zion's Watch Tower*, March 1883); 1897 (*Zion's Watch Tower*, 1 June 1897, 161).

[4] *Jehovah's Witnesses in the Divine Purpose* (Brooklyn: Watchtower Bible and Tract Society of New York, 1959), 140.

[5] Ibid.

the Lamb's scroll of life [will]" (21:27). So if one's name *is* in the book or scroll of life, one enters heaven. If it is not, the lake of fire awaits. There is no room for another class.

The Watchtower also teaches that only the 144,000 "anointed" are born again: "Born again means a birth-like realization of prospects and hopes for spirit life by resurrection to heaven."[6] This particular understanding of being "born again" is foreign to Scripture. John writes, "Everyone believing that Jesus is the Christ has been born from God" (1 John 5:1).[7] Jesus also said, "unless anyone is born from water and spirit, he cannot enter into the kingdom of God. . . . *You people must be born again*" (John 3:5–7; emphasis added). Jesus did not add, "But that only applies to 144,000 of you. The rest *cannot* enter into the kingdom of God."

The conclusion is inescapable: If one is not born again, he cannot enter the kingdom of God. If one does not enter the kingdom of God, Scripture indicates, not that paradise awaits him, but rather the wailing and "grinding of teeth" reserved for the unrighteous (Matt. 8:11–12, 1 Cor. 6:9). The Bible is clear in that a person is either born again and thus enters the kingdom of God, or he is not born again and consequently is "thrown into the darkness outside" (Matt. 8:12).

Reiterating Christ's teaching, Paul exhorts the Christian community to remember that "our citizenship exists in the heavens" (Phil. 3:20). He mentions this fact again when addressing the Corinthians: "For we know that if our earthly house, this tent, should be dissolved, we are to have a building from God, a house . . . everlasting in the heavens" (2 Cor. 5:1). Numerous other verses demonstrate that Christians go to heaven, including Hebrews 3:1; Ephesians 2:6; Colossians 1:4, 5; and 1 Peter 1:4. Witnesses often retort that Paul is speaking to the anointed class that has a heavenly hope, not to those with an earthly hope. But this is

---

[6] *Make Sure of All Things* (Brooklyn: Watchtower Bible and Tract Society of New York, 1953), 48.

[7] See also John 1:12 and 1 John 3:1, 2 for further evidence that all Christians are born again.

not supported by the text. Paul is emphatic in stating that just as there is one body, there is one hope to which all are called (Eph. 4:4). His letters were not written to a select few but to "all who everywhere are calling upon the name of the Lord, Jesus Christ" (1 Cor. 1:2).

Regarding those who supposedly have only an earthly hope, the Watchtower attempts to use verses such as Psalm 37:29 as evidence that the just are to inherit the land forever, and it understands "land" to mean the earth. In context, this verse refers to inheriting the Promised Land as a sign of God's blessing in the Old Testament. Hebrews 11:8–16 indicates that there is a homeland better than the Promised Land on earth, and this is the heavenly one for those who die in faith. Along these lines, the Old Testament patriarchs "publicly declared that they were strangers and temporary residents in the land. . . . They are earnestly seeking a place of their own. . . . But now they are reaching out for a better [place], that is, one belonging to heaven. . . . God . . . has made a city ready for them." (Heb. 11:13–16)

These Old Testament men and women "did not get the [fulfillment of the] promise . . . as God foresaw something better for us." (Heb. 11:39–40)

Perhaps unaware of the implications of its own statements, the Watchtower goes so far as to say about this passage, "Who are here meant by 'us'? Hebrews 3:1 shows that they are 'partakers of the heavenly calling.' "[8] Even the NWT footnote makes clear that the "city" in these verses is the *heavenly* Jerusalem mentioned in Hebrews 12:22 and Revelation 21:2.

Despite overwhelming biblical evidence, the Watchtower refuses to acknowledge that anyone who lived before Christ will ever enter heaven: "The Apostle Paul in the eleventh chapter of Hebrews names a long list of faithful men who died before the crucifixion of the Lord. . . . These can never be a part of the

---

[8] *Reasoning from the Scriptures*, 78.

heavenly class. . . . [T]hey had no heavenly hopes."[9] Thus, "the pre-Christian persons who had faith, then, must have a hope for the perfect life somewhere other than in heaven."[10] In light of the biblical evidence, it is impossible for any Witness to explain how one can be a partaker of the heavenly calling and have the heavenly Jerusalem prepared for him by God without the hope of ever going to heaven.

Is heaven really closed to those who lived before the death of Christ? Matthew 8:11–12 counters such a theory, since Jesus proclaims that "many from eastern parts and western parts will come and recline at the table *with Abraham and Isaac and Jacob in the kingdom of the heavens*" (emphasis added). In keeping with the Watchtower's interpretation, though, *The Greatest Man Who Ever Lived*, a text often used in the weekly book study at Kingdom Halls, states that there are 144,000 individuals in God's "heavenly Kingdom."[11] But Matthew 8 makes it clear that Abraham, Isaac, and Jacob are indeed in the "kingdom of the heavens." Nonetheless, the Witnesses are forced to argue that they cannot be in heaven, since the Watchtower teaches that these individuals have only the earthly hope. This is a clear example of Witnesses being compelled to choose between the authority of the Watchtower and that of Scripture, as one is certainly in error. Unfortunately, Witnesses will most often refuse to acknowledge the discrepancy, in spite of clear-cut biblical evidence.

Further, Matthew 5:5 says, "Happy are the mild-tempered ones, since they will inherit the earth." Indeed the mild-tempered will inherit a new earth, just as the pure in heart will see God, the peaceable will be called sons of God, and the persecuted ones will possess the kingdom of the heavens. These blessings are all ad-

---

[9] *Millions Now Living Will Never Die* (Brooklyn: Watchtower Bible and Tract Society of New York, 1920), 89.

[10] *Reasoning from the Scriptures*, 78.

[11] *The Greatest Man Who Ever Lived* (Brooklyn: Watchtower Bible and Tract Society of New York, 1991), chap. 83.

dressed to one and the same audience. Jesus was not implying that if a person is mild-tempered, he will live on earth forever, whereas the persecuted will reside in a different locale for all eternity.

When discussing the concepts of heaven, earth, and the 144,000 with a Witness, do not aim to show how all believers will be in heaven rather than on earth. Instead, acknowledge that the New Jerusalem will descend and heaven will be on the new earth. There will indeed be a new heaven and a new earth, and the bride of Christ will be one flock. The earth as we know it will "wear out" (Is. 51:6) and "pass away" (Matt. 24:35), giving rise to a new heaven and a new earth (Rev. 21:1). Likewise, Peter makes no distinction between these two hopes but combines them as one new creation:

> [T]he heavens being on fire will be dissolved and the elements being intensely hot will melt! But there are new heavens and a new earth that we are awaiting according to his promise, and in these righteousness is to dwell. Hence, beloved ones . . . you are awaiting these things. (2 Pet. 3:12–14)

The Witnesses often point out that God originally made man to live on earth, and they therefore ask, "Why would he do that if he intended for us to live in heaven?" The answer to this question is provided by John in Revelation 21:1–5, 7, 8:

> And I saw a new heaven and a new earth; for the former heaven and the former earth had passed away, and the sea is no more. I saw also the holy city, New Jerusalem, coming down out of heaven from God and prepared as a bride adorned for her husband. With that I heard a loud voice from the throne say: "Look! The tent of God is with mankind, and he will reside with them, and they will be his peoples. And God himself will be with them. And he will wipe out every tear from their eyes, and death will be no more, neither will mourning nor outcry nor pain be anymore. The former things have passed away."
>
> And the One seated on the throne said: "Look! I am making all things new." . . . Anyone conquering will inherit these things, and I shall be his God and he will be my son. But as for the cowards

and those without faith . . . their portion will be in the lake that burns with fire and sulphur."

What, then, is the proper understanding of these passages? The *Catechism of the Catholic Church* explains:

> Sacred Scripture calls this mysterious renewal, which will transform humanity and the world, "new heavens and a new earth" [2 Pet. 3:13]. It will be the definitive realization of God's plan to bring under a single head "all things in [Christ], things in heaven and things on earth" [Eph. 1:10].
>
> In this new universe, the heavenly Jerusalem, God will have his dwelling among men. "He will wipe away every tear from their eyes, and death shall be no more, neither shall there be mourning nor crying nor pain any more, for the former things have passed away" [Rev. 21:4].
>
> The visible universe, then, is itself destined to be transformed, so that the world itself, restored to its original state, facing no further obstacles, should be at the service of the just, sharing their glorification in the risen Jesus Christ.[12]

God does plan on making all things new. Jehovah's Witnesses do well in acknowledging that a new earth does play a role in the fulfillment of God's creation—renewing the universe. When speaking with them, affirm this truth and acknowledge that too many overlook it. They are not wrong in saying that many will live forever in paradise on earth. Where they fall into error is in saying that some of the saved will be only in heaven for all eternity and not on the new earth. Scripture indicates that the two will be one in God's new creation. If anything, the Witnesses err in saying that too many stay in a separate heaven!

When discussing these points with Witnesses, remind them that they were created to see the face of God, as David was: "As the deer longs for streams of water, so my soul longs for you, O God. My being thirsts for God, the living God. When can I go and see the face of God?" (Ps. 42; NAB). The understanding of paradise

---

[12] CCC 1043–44, 1047.

that is communicated by the Watchtower, depicted in its literature by idyllic illustrations of people cuddling with lions and other animals, falls far short of what God has told us he has intended for us—the glory of the Beatific Vision.

12

Is the Soul Immortal?

*The apostate doctrine of the immortality of the soul is another of Christen-
dom's unscriptural traditions stemming from Greek philosophy. "For the
living are conscious that they will die; but as for the dead, they are conscious
of nothing at all" (Eccl. 9:5). A man does not have an immortal soul—he
is a soul, and that soul ceases to exist when the body dies.[1] The doctrine
of the inherent immortality of the soul is the main one that the devil has
used down through the ages to deceive people and hold them in bondage to
religion.*

The English word *soul* is a translation of the Hebrew word
nephesh and the Greek word *psuchē*. These two words appear approximately nine hundred times in the course of the Old and
New Testaments, and they have an extraordinarily wide range
of meaning, as illustrated by the variety of things Scripture says
concerning the soul. For example, one's soul can go out at death
(Gen. 35:18) and come back within (1 Kgs. 17:21). The person
is called a soul (Gen. 2:7) and has a soul (Luke 1:46). But there is
a distinction between body, soul, and spirit (1 Thess. 5:23), since
the soul is distinct from the body (Matt. 10:28). The soul can
die, suffocate, and be killed by a sword (Job 7:15, Josh. 10:37);
it can also live and speak after death (Rev. 6:9–11), and it cannot
be killed by man (Matt. 10:28).

With such a diverse range of statements, one would err in thinking that the definition of the term could be summed up by any
particular verse or that one definition could fit all verses. For ex-

---

[1] *Reasoning from the Scriptures* (Brooklyn: Watchtower Bible and Tract Society of New York, 1985), 375–80.

ample, the term is sometimes used to designate the spiritual part of a human being (which cannot be killed), but sometimes it is used to refer to the whole human being (which can be killed by the separation of its physical and spiritual parts).

The main passage used by Witnesses to buttress their idea that the person is not conscious after death is Ecclesiastes 9:5–6, which says of the dead that "they are conscious of nothing at all, neither do they anymore have wages, because the remembrance of them has been forgotten" and that "they have no portion anymore to time indefinite in anything that has to be done under the sun."

Notice that the first sentence denies that anyone remembers the dead. This is obviously not true, but it fits with the author's use of hyperbole in discussing his theme of the vanity of life. Reading on, the last sentence, if read literally, could be construed as denying the resurrection of the body to a life under the sun—a teaching that no Witness would deny.

These two sentences can be used to explain to Witnesses that the sacred author is merely explaining the way he sees things, not laying the foundation for a definitive theological explanation of the afterlife. He is only speaking of how the dead appear to those on earth. He is using phenomenological language—the language of how things *appear*, not of how they necessarily *are*.[2] From an outer, earthly perspective, the dead (i.e., the bodies they leave behind on earth) do not appear to be conscious of anything, do not earn wages, and no longer have a part in the affairs of human society "under the sun." Witnesses often assert that churches of Christendom pull verses out of context, but this is one place where the finger clearly points back at them.

It must also be noted that the Old Testament writers did not have a complete understanding of the condition of the dead. For instance, Job 7:9 reads: "So he that is going down to She'ol will not come up." This seems to deny the resurrection of the body,

---

[2] A classic example of phenomenological language is when we speak of the sun rising and setting. It appears to rise and set, though this appearance is actually generated primarily by the motion of the earth.

which is clearly taught in the New Testament. For this reason, it is very dangerous to hang an entire doctrine on such scant biblical evidence, especially when it concerns teachings that were not fully understood or fully revealed before Christ.

In the Old Testament, the prophet Isaiah speaks of the condition of the dead when he says, "She'ol underneath has become agitated at you in order to meet you on coming in. . . . It has made all the kings of the nations get up from their thrones. All of them speak up and say to you, 'Have you yourself also been made weak like us?' " (Is. 14:9–10) and "Those seeing you will gaze even at you; they will give close examination even to you, [saying,] 'Is this the man that was agitating the earth, that was making kingdoms rock, that made the productive land like the wilderness and that overthrew its very cities, that did not open the way homeward even for his prisoners?' " (Is. 14:16–17; brackets in original).

Again, we see the dead talking to the dead in the next world. Elsewhere in the Old Testament, long after the prophet Samuel had died, he appeared to Saul and conversed with him (1 Sam. 28). These two passages indicate clearly that the dead are conscious, and the New Testament tells the same story.

Perhaps the strongest contradiction of the Watchtower doctrine is seen in Christ's descent to hades. In 1 Peter 3:19, the apostle tells his readers how Jesus "preached to the spirits in prison." If the dead were unconscious, then his preaching would have been futile. The Watchtower replies that these "spirits" are not disembodied souls but disobedient spirits (angels), to whom Jesus preached a message of judgment.

However, the difficulty with such an interpretation arises a chapter later, when Peter explains that "the good news was declared also to the dead" (1 Pet. 4:6). Angels do not die, and once they have fallen there is no point in bringing them the gospel. This passage does not refer to angels or to the spiritually dead but to those who are just plain dead. If it referred to the spiritually dead, Peter would not have said that the good news had "also" been brought to them. That would imply that the primary recipients of the gospel were those who were already spiritually alive, but the first-century proclamation of the gospel was to bring spiritual life *to* people. Also, the context renders the Watchtower's interpretation impossible, since it speaks of the judgment of the living and the dead. The NWT footnotes on the passage even direct the reader to Revelation 20:12, which explicitly notes that the dead are those who have literally died. At this point, a Witness may change the topic to the nature of death: "We need to define what death is. When you die, you cease to exist. So Jesus could not be preaching to the dead." Back to square one? Press on.

Paul declared, "For in my case to live is Christ, and to die, gain" (Phil. 1:21) and that "what I do desire is the releasing and the being with Christ, for this, to be sure, is far better" (1:23). If death is unconsciousness, Paul would not consider it gain. It is clear that he sees death as enabling us "to become absent from the body and to make our home with the Lord" (2 Cor. 5:8).

During the Transfiguration, Jesus conversed with Moses and Elijah (Mark 9:4). If they were not conscious, Jesus could not have conversed with them. A Witness will therefore be forced to argue that Moses and Elijah were not really there, since they were still unconscious in the grave. Apparently God was just making them *seem* to appear to Peter, James, and John—an idea that is absurd, since God clearly would not misrepresent the nature of existence beyond the grave or mislead someone to think that people are conscious after death when they are not.

Another passage that gives the Witnesses difficulty is the story of Lazarus and the rich man in Luke 16:19–31. Witnesses will probably offer one of two possible explanations for this story. First, Witnesses will suggest an interpretation that is highly speculative and depends wholly upon the teachings of the Watchtower. For instance, Witnesses claim that Lazarus represents a *class* of people who are *spiritual* beggars, whereas the rich man represents the *class* of hypocritical Jewish religious leaders (i.e., the Scribes, the Pharisees, and the Sadducees). The story then becomes a matter of the Lazarus class's no longer depending on the rich-man class once Jesus appears on the scene:

Thus the Lazarus class had died to the Mosaic law and was no longer subject to the "rich man" class or dependent upon that Jewish clergy class for anything. They had "died together with Christ toward the elementary things of the world" which the "rich man" class taught. Their life was now "hidden with the Christ in union with God." They no longer begged from the "rich man." No, they followed Jesus' command, "Watch out for the yeast of the Pharisees, which is hypocrisy," and avoided them.[3]

Continuing this unique interpretation, the Watchtower offers its explanation of the meaning of Abraham's bosom in the story:

> To be carried by angels into Abraham's bosom means, therefore, to be transferred from the despised beggarly condition of Lazarus at the rich man's gate into the loving favor of the Greater Abraham, Jehovah God. It means to be adopted by him as a son of God to be associated with the promised Seed of Abraham, Jesus Christ.[4]

Of course, there is nothing in this Gospel account of Lazarus even to intimate that such an interpretation is correct. The Watchtower's understanding here necessarily involves a distortion of the plain sense of the text, as it needs to reinterpret Scripture to fit its own theological system.

Second, Witnesses will claim that this story is a parable and should not be taken literally. Even granting that this story is a parable, the question still arises as to why Jesus would use this story to teach if, from the Watchtower's point of view, it is actually an impossible scenario. In other words, why would Jesus explain that the dead are conscious if, in fact, they are not? This would be like telling a parable about a man who was reincarnated. Undaunted, however, the Watchtower claims, "This doctrine [of the inherent immortality of the soul] is the main one that the Devil has used down through the ages to deceive the people and

---

[3] *The Watchtower*, 15 February 1951, 123. This interpretation is still held by the Watchtower organization (cf. *The Watchtower*, 1 April 1989, 24–25.)

[4] Ibid., 124.

hold them in bondage to Religion."[5] But if the soul's immortality is such a diabolical doctrine, why does Jesus use an example of it as the foundation for one of his teachings?

A great deal of the New Testament evidence for the soul's immortality and conscious existence after death can be found in the book of Revelation. Souls do live past the death of the bodies: John "saw underneath the altar [in heaven] the souls of those slaughtered because of the word of God and because of the witness work that they used to have. And they cried with a loud voice" (6:9–10). Because the soul does not die with the flesh, those in heaven are able to offer prayers to God (5:8) and live in happiness (14:13). A Witness will be forced to admit that there are souls existing apart from their bodies, but he will attempt to add the caveat that these are some of the 144,000. But reading chapters five to seven of Revelation successively, one sees that the 144,000 were still on earth while the souls of the martyrs in heaven cried out.

Another way the Watchtower attempts to deny the soul's immortality is to observe that Scripture speaks of dead people as being "asleep." Now it's true that the Bible uses such a description, but it uses the term *sleep* to refer to the state of the dead because that is the appearance of their bodies, not the state of their consciousness. It is noteworthy that the term *sleep* in the Bible is always in reference to the body, never to the soul. Again, we have the language of appearances. Dead bodies *appear* to be sleeping people.

Still more problems are created for the Watchtower position by other verses. For example, the body is described as just a tent, or tabernacle, that does not last (2 Cor. 5:1–4; 2 Pet. 1:13), compared to the essential self (or soul), which does. Further, Jesus tells us that man cannot kill the soul (Matt. 10:28). If a soul is simply a living body, then Witnesses must conclude that men cannot kill a living body. When this is pointed out, they may retreat to the position of saying that the soul is really the life of one in the mem-

---

[5] *Let God Be True* (Brooklyn: Watchtower Bible and Tract Society of New York, 1946), 66.

ory of God, and that is what men cannot kill. Such a definition still is unable to explain how this soul is able to cry out and listen without its body (Rev. 6:9–11).

13

Is Hell Real?

Everlasting punishment is a myth and a lie invented by Satan. Hell is merely mankind's common grave, and it is assuredly not a fiery torture. Such a cruel idea is from ancient Babylonian, Egyptian, Buddhist, and Assyrian beliefs. The Bible teaches us that hell is a place where the dead are conscious of nothing, obviously feeling no pain. As Pastor Russell recognized from the outset, the doctrine of hellfire is unscriptural, unreasonable, and contrary to God's mercy. Doesn't the Bible say that God is love (1 John 4:8)? The Bible says that Job wanted to be protected in hell (Job 14:13), and that the dead will be delivered from hell (Rev. 20:13). But eternal torment can hardly be considered a place of protection, and Christendom teaches that no one will be delivered from it. Thus Christendom's doctrine of hellfire is unbiblical.[1]

One of the most important considerations when discussing the topic of hell with Witnesses is the fact that the word has carried different meanings over time. Today the word *hell* is equated with the fiery place of the damned, and the Witnesses are right in pointing out that this is not the historic meaning of the term. In prior eras, *hell* merely indicated the place of the dead, which is the original meaning of the German word *Hoelle*, from which the English *hell* is derived. In a similar fashion, Witnesses begin on the right foot by acknowledging that the Greek word *hadēs* ("hades") and the Hebrew word *shᵉ'ōl* ("sheol") do not unequivocally refer to a place of torture. *Hadēs* and *shᵉ'ōl*, like the original meaning of

---

[1] *Let God Be True* (Brooklyn: Watchtower Bible and Tract Society of New York, 1952), 88–99; *Reasoning from the Scriptures* (Brooklyn: Watchtower Bible and Tract Society of New York, 1985), 168–75.

the word *hell,* simply meant "the place of the dead." That is why Job wished to be there and why the dead will be delivered from it.

Thus, in the Apostles' Creed, the Church affirms that Jesus descended into hell, though he was never in the place of the damned. The *Catechism of the Catholic Church* explains:

> Scripture calls the abode of the dead, to which the dead Christ went down, "hell"—*Sheol* in Hebrew or *Hades* in Greek—because those who are there are deprived of the vision of God. Such is the case for all the dead, whether evil or righteous, while they await the redeemer: which does not mean that their lot is identical, as Jesus shows through the parable of the poor man Lazarus who was received into "Abraham's bosom": It is precisely these holy souls, who awaited their Savior in Abraham's bosom, whom Christ the Lord delivered when he descended into hell. Jesus did not descend into hell to deliver the damned, nor to destroy the hell of damnation, but to free the just who had gone before him.[2]

Since *hell* has traditionally meant the place of the dead, the Witnesses capitalize on the modern alteration of its definition and conclude that hellfire is therefore an unbiblical invention. Does Scripture warrant such a conclusion? No. Rather, it says that the damned "shall be tormented with fire and sulfur . . . the smoke of their torment ascends forever and ever, and day and night they have no rest" (Rev. 14:10–11). When faced with this passage, the Witness is forced to conclude that it cannot refer to conscious torment, since the Watchtower teaches that the dead are not conscious.

Moving behind the English, the Greek word for torment is *basanizō*, which refers only to punishment, torment, or vexation, not to annihilation and unconsciousness (cf. Matt. 8:6, 29; Mark 5:7; Luke 8:28). There is no reference in Scripture to unconscious torment, as it is a contradiction in terms. Therefore, the idea of hellfire is not "a myth invented by Satan," as the Watchtower asserts; rather it is an "everlasting fire prepared for the Devil and his

---

[2] CCC 633.

angels" (Matt. 25:41), a "lake of fire and sulphur, where . . . they
will be tormented day and night, forever and ever" (Rev. 20:10).

In another Bible passage dealing with conscious torment after
death, Jesus tells his listeners of Lazarus and the rich man:

> [T]he beggar died and he was carried off by the angels to the bo-
> som [position] of Abraham. Also the rich man died and was buried.
> And in Hades he lifted up his eyes, he existing in torments, and
> he saw Abraham afar off and Lazarus in the bosom [position] with
> him. So he called and said, "Father Abraham, have mercy on me
> and send Lazarus to dip the tip of his finger in water and cool my
> tongue, because I am in anguish in this blazing fire." (Luke 16:22–
> 24; brackets around "position" in original)

Though Luke never identifies this story as a parable, the Watchtower maintains that it is a metaphor. What it represents, Watchtower sources do not agree upon. In *Reasoning from the Scriptures*,
for example, the suffering of the rich man is said to represent
the torment the Jews underwent when given the judgment messages in the book of Acts (5:33; 7:54). The Watchtower, however,
reads the following into the text: "The rich man represents the
ultraselfish class of the clergy of Christendom, who are now afar
off from God and dead to his favor and service and tormented
by the Kingdom truth proclaimed."[3] These ideas—so foreign to
the commonsense interpretation of the passage—show to what
lengths the Watchtower goes to explain away the biblical evidence for eternal torment.

Jesus stated that the place of the damned is likened to Gehenna,
which was previously the center of an idolatrous cult that offered
children as sacrifices. This "Valley of Hinnom" was located south-
east of Jerusalem and was used in the first century as a garbage
dump where trash was burned day and night. Our Lord informs his
listeners that the place of the damned is like that, a place "where
the maggot does not die, and the fire is not put out" (Mark 9:48).
It is the place where the wicked are sent, and from this "everlast-

---

[3] *Let God Be True*, 98.

ing fire" (Matt. 18:8) will come "weeping and the gnashing of [their] teeth" (Matt. 8:12).

In contrast to this, the Watchtower argues that, "Living humans were not pitched into Gehenna; so it was not a place of conscious torment."[4] However, this line of reasoning does not come from Scripture, which indicates the opposite in Revelation 19:20: "*While still alive*, they both [the beast and the false prophet] were hurled into the fiery lake that burns with sulphur" (emphasis and brackets added). While there can be everlasting fire without conscious torment (as if corpses were being incinerated), there can be no "wailing and grinding of teeth" without consciousness.

If the damned are unconscious, as the Watchtower contends, it is absurd that Jesus would choose such contradictory illustrations as Gehenna and the rich man in flames to convey this. If anguish and torment after death are not real, it becomes difficult to maintain that the above passages symbolically represent that the wicked after death are unconscious and not in pain.

In every biblical account of the final separation of the wicked and the just, the consciousness of both parties is presumed: "There is where [your] weeping and the gnashing of [your] teeth will be, when you see Abraham and Isaac and Jacob and all the prophets in the kingdom of God, but yourselves thrown outside" (Luke 13:28; brackets in original; cf. Matt. 8:11–12). There is no indication that the first group is conscious, while the second is not. Rather, Jesus emphasizes the consciousness of the damned.

Another classical objection to eternal torment is the appeal to the love of God. People espousing this belief maintain that God's love precludes the possibility of his allowing any creature to be tormented eternally. But does God's love actually prohibit the existence of suffering in the afterlife? The answer is no, because if the existence of suffering in this life does not detract from the fact that God is love, neither does suffering in the next life. If anything, the goodness of God would seem to be more challenged by the suffering of the innocent in this life than by the punishment of

---

[4] Ibid., 173.

the wicked in the next (though even that does not challenge his goodness, since God will simply compensate the innocent in the next life for what they suffered in this one).

God is love, and he offers his presence and love to anyone who will accept it. Should individuals refuse this proposal, God honors their choice and gives them what *they* asked for—eternity apart from his presence and love. "Eternal damnation" is not God's initiative; he desires the salvation of all. Rather, hell is the reality of people's refusal of God's love—and continuing to do so after death. If the damned were to repent, they would be accepted by God. But at death the will becomes fixed, either on good or evil, so the lost remain lost because they continue to choose to reject God's love. Consequently, God is not to blame for people's choices, and his goodness is not impugned because some refuse to accept him.

But what of the claims that eternal damnation is a teaching that originated with the ancient Babylonians and other pagans? It is worth noting that the doctrine of an eternal paradise to come was also held by many pagan religions. Thus one could argue that if the doctrine of eternal damnation is false because pagans believed it, then an afterlife paradise must, by the same token, be a pagan myth. This reveals a fundamental problem with much of the Witnesses' teaching. They often denounce things as being pagan in origin, but they do so only selectively. When they want to denounce a Christian concept (e.g., eternal torment), they accuse it of being pagan, based on parallels in other religions. But when they want to keep a Christian concept (e.g., eternal paradise), they do not denounce it as pagan even when there are parallels in other religions.[5] Often the pagan parallels that Witnesses cite simply aren't there. For example, the Babylonians did not believe in an eternal fiery punishment. As *The Epic of Gilgamesh* reveals,

---

[5] For more information on accusations of paganism, see James Akin, "The Pagan Influence Fallacy," *This Rock* (March 2000), 39–41; "Tracking the First Pagans," *This Rock* (November 1999), 38–39; and "The Woman, the Seed, the Serpent," *This Rock* (October 1999), 39–40.

their concept of the afterlife was bleak, but it is altogether different from the idea of hell. For the Babylonians, the afterlife is bleak for *everyone*, there being no distinction between the saved and the damned.

That many ancient cultures knew of punishment in the afterlife only strengthens the case for the teaching. It demonstrates that human nature knows that it is contrary to God's justice for sin to go unpunished. To simply withhold the reward of paradise by leaving the damned unconscious forever is no real punishment, since they are not aware of anything.

For the sake of argument, suppose that Hitler is damned. Would not the justice of God require that he receive a worse punishment than an eternity of rest for torturing and killing millions? Beyond that, do all of the damned deserve the same punishment? Scripture indicates that, just as there are degrees of glory, there are degrees of punishment (Matt. 11:20–24). Some will be beaten more severely than others (Luke 12:48). But this cannot be the case if death and damnation amount to annihilation, for there are no degrees of nonexistence.

14

What about Military Service, Blood Transfusions, and Holidays?

Military Service

The allegiance of the Jehovah's Witness is to God, not to man. A person is to serve in one army—Jehovah's—and to follow only his leadership. For this reason, saluting the flag of any nation is idolatry.[1] One is not to vote, run for office, and especially not to enter military service. Jesus said to turn the other cheek, not to kill nation after nation. All war is displeasing to God, if everyone in the world were a Jehovah's Witness, there would be no war.

Beginning with the last argument first, it does not follow that if everyone were a Jehovah's Witness there would be no war. Only if everyone lived by the Watchtower doctrine on war would there be no war, but the same could be said if everyone were Catholic and lived by the Ten Commandments.

One gaping hole in the Witnesses' argument against war (or joining the military) is that the Bible and Jesus never condemned it as always wrong. Christ's command to turn the other cheek was a personal exhortation for how the Christian should deal with personal injury; it was not a denial of the government's freedom and duty to protect its citizens from unjust foreign aggression. The Lord had several encounters with soldiers, but he never instructed them to abandon their occupation. On the contrary, in Matthew

---

[1] *Let God Be True* (Brooklyn: Watchtower Bible and Tract Society of New York, 1952), 243.

8:10 he praises a Roman centurion for his faith. Cornelius was also a Roman centurion (the equivalent of an army captain) and the first regular Gentile to be a member of the Church (Acts 10:24–48). Even the NWT records that he was an "army officer, a man righteous and fearing God" (Acts 10:22). In Luke 3:14, the greatest of prophets of the Old Covenant, John the Baptist, had the ideal opportunity to denounce the military, but he does nothing of the sort: "Also those in military service would ask him: 'What shall we also do?' And he said to them: 'Do not harass anybody or accuse anybody falsely, but be satisfied with YOUR provisions.' " The New Testament simply does not provide any evidence for the Watchtower's position, and the Old Testament is replete with battles being fought at the command of God.

While unjust violence is indeed contrary to God's laws, the Bible never condemns war that is waged for a just reason. That is why God led Israel into numerous battles in the Old Testament. If war were intrinsically evil, God would have had no part of it. Thus, some wars are clearly just, since God himself backed them. So the question then becomes, "When is war justified?" The *Catechism of the Catholic Church* says this:

> Legitimate defense can be not only a right but a grave duty for one who is responsible for the lives of others. The defense of the common good requires that an unjust aggressor be rendered unable to cause harm. For this reason, those who legitimately hold authority also have the right to use arms to repel aggressors against the civil community entrusted to their responsibility.
>
> The strict conditions for legitimate defense by military force require rigorous consideration. The gravity of such a decision makes it subject to rigorous conditions of moral legitimacy. At one and the same time:
>   —the damage inflicted by the aggressor on the nation or community of nations must be lasting, grave, and certain;
>   —all other means of putting an end to it must have been shown to be impractical or ineffective;
>   —there must be serious prospects of success;
>   —the use of arms must not produce evils and disorders graver

than the evil to be eliminated. The power of modern means of destruction weighs very heavily in evaluating this condition.

These are the traditional elements enumerated in what is called the "just war" doctrine.

The evaluation of these conditions for moral legitimacy belongs to the prudential judgment of those who have responsibility for the common good.

Injustice, excessive economic or social inequalities, envy, distrust, and pride raging among men and nations constantly threaten peace and cause wars. Everything done to overcome these disorders contributes to building up peace and avoiding war:

Insofar as men are sinners, the threat of war hangs over them and will so continue until Christ comes again; but insofar as they can vanquish sin by coming together in charity, violence itself will be vanquished and these words will be fulfilled: "they shall beat their swords into plowshares, and their spears into pruning hooks; nation shall not lift up sword against nation, neither shall they learn war any more."[2]

Though some find the passivism and neutrality of the Witnesses appealing, they do not often think through its consequences. If a Kingdom Hall were mobbed, would the men of the congregation have any right to use force to defend the women and children from being murdered by the assailants? Of course they would. On a larger scale, that same moral principle of defending the innocent is the proper use of the armed forces. The solution to any present injustices is to ensure the proper use of force, not to take away the power itself, for the abuse of a thing does not take away its proper use. Further, Scripture does not consider it a virtuous thing for a person to watch the innocent suffer while he has the power to stop the injustice. God himself said this:

If you remain indifferent in time of adversity, your strength will depart from you. Rescue those that are being dragged to death, and from those tottering to execution, withdraw not. If you say, "I know not this man," does not he who tests hearts perceive it? He

---

[2] CCC, 2265, 2309, 2317; cf. *Gaudium et Spes* 78 §6, quoting Is. 2:4.

who guards your life knows it, and he will repay each one according to his deeds. (Prov. 24:10–12; NAB)

Blood Transfusions

The Bible forbids eating blood (Gen. 9:4; Lev. 17:10–15), and this includes blood transfusions. The apostle James commanded us to "abstain from meat sacrificed to idols, from blood, from meats of strangled animals" (Acts 15:20, 29). "It is a statute to time indefinite for your generations, in all your dwelling places: You must not eat any fat or any blood at all" (Lev. 3:17). One temporarily prolongs his earthly life at the cost of his eternal life if he has a blood transfusion.[3]

Since documented evidence of the practice of blood transfusion cannot be found until Europeans attempted it in the mid-seventeenth century,[4] it cannot be said that the Bible condemns the practice. But can an argument be made that Scripture lays down general moral principles that would forbid such a procedure?

The Old Testament provides several laws against the oral consumption of blood, for example in Leviticus 17. When a Witness cites any precept of the Mosaic Law, however, it should immediately be noted that Christians are no longer bound by it. If Christians were, they would have to obey the entire chapter of Leviticus 17, which commands the sacrifice of ox, sheep, and goats and the burning of their fat before the Lord. If one eats an animal that was found dead or was killed by other animals, the Christian would have to bathe in water and be ritually unclean until evening. Sandwiched between these Mosaic precepts is the rule that the Israelites are not to partake of blood. For this reason, today's Orthodox Jews eat only Kosher foods. These Jews are strict followers of the Mosaic Law, yet they allow blood transfusion.

---

[3] *Reasoning from the Scriptures* (Brooklyn: Watchtower Bible and Tract Society of New York, 1985), 70–76; *Blood, Medicine, and the Law of God* (Brooklyn: Watchtower Bible and Tract Society of New York, 1961), 55.

[4] See *Encyclopedia Brittanica*, s.v. "Blood Transfusion," at *www.brittanica.com*.

The Old Testament-based arguments for a prohibition of blood transfusion are simple to address, but one must also explain the words of James at the Council of Jerusalem, which the Watchtower uses to support its teaching on blood. After Peter addresses the doctrinal matter of the salvation of Gentiles and Jews, James responds by adding pastoral suggestions that the Gentiles should be told to "abstain from things polluted by idols, and from fornication[5] and from what is strangled and from blood" (Acts 15:20).

These were disciplinary measures that James proposed to avoid causing scandal to Jewish converts to Christianity. As Paul says, "I know and am persuaded in the Lord Jesus that nothing is defiled in itself; only where a man considers something to be defiled, to him it is defiled. . . . True, all things are clean. . . . It is not well to eat flesh or to drink wine or do anything over which your brother stumbles" (Rom. 14:14, 20, 21).

If it were intrinsically immoral for a person to consume blood, Jesus would not have told his followers to drink his blood (Matt. 26:27–28, Mark 14:23–24, Luke 22:20, John 6:54–55). Even if his words were merely symbolic—which they weren't—his holiness would prevent him from telling the faithful to recall his act of redemption by symbolically performing an inherently sinful act. To do so would be as absurd as commanding the disciples to perform a ritual symbolizing adultery to remember the fidelity of God.

In addition to these considerations, the Watchtower itself has not been consistent throughout its history regarding blood. For example, it used to condemn vaccinations, the use of blood fractions,[6] and organ transplants. Now these practices are often allowed,[7] and no one can be certain how many lives have been

---

[5] As a side note, the NWT rendering of the Greek word *porneia* as "fornication" is a poor translation. In this particular context it refers to marriages that are considered unlawful by Jewish standards.

[6] For example, blood plasma. See *How Can Blood Save Your Life?* (Brooklyn: Watchtower Bible and Tract Society of New York, 1990), 27.

[7] Vaccinations and organ transplants are commonly allowed, as are some uses of blood fractions, or components of whole blood. A footnote to *How*

needlessly lost as a result of the Watchtower's false teachings prohibiting them. Moreover, if one cannot trust the organization with one's temporal life, how much less with one's eternal life!

Holidays

Celebrating holidays is simply not a biblical practice. The only two mentions of birthdays in the Scriptures—Pharaoh's in Genesis 40 and Herod's in Matthew 14—are not pleasing to God. So the celebrations should be shunned. These give glory to people and not to God. They are of pagan origin and must be displeasing to Jehovah. Easter is clearly pagan, being celebrated on the first full moon after the Spring equinox. Easter is nothing else than Astarte/Ishtar, the Assyrian queen goddess of heaven. Christmas is never celebrated in the Bible, and we should not add pagan traditions to Scripture.[8]

Birthdays and Paganism

There's plenty to cover here, but we can begin by examining the idea that God is dishonored if creatures are honored. While it is entirely true that idolatry displeases the Lord, it could not be further from the truth to assert that the honoring of man dishonors God. When one looks in the book of Revelation, for instance, it is clear that the Lord delights in glorifying his children and bestowing upon them crowns and thrones that they might have a share in his glory (4:4). Paul also says something relevant in his first letter to the Corinthians: "if a member is glorified, all the other members rejoice with it" (1 Cor. 12:26). If both the Lord and St. Paul take such delight in the honoring of members of the

---

Can Blood Save Your Life? says that "Witnesses do not accept transfusions of whole blood, red cells, white cells, platelets, or blood plasma. As to minor fractions, such as immune globulin, see *The Watchtower* of June 1, 1990, pages 30–1."

[8] *Reasoning from the Scriptures*, 68–70, 176–82.

body of Christ, one should have no qualms about celebrating such a thing as the gift of life that God has given.

When birthdays are mentioned in Scripture, the celebrations themselves are not condemned. There is not one word in Scripture saying that either of the two birthday celebrations mentioned was bad or should not have taken place.

In the case of Pharaoh's birthday, there is nothing critical of the celebration. Neither is there anything critical of Pharaoh's actions on the day. It does mention that he had one of his former servants put to death on that day, but Scripture is silent about whether the man had done anything worthy of death. That question is not considered, and we are given no information about what the servant had done that led him first to be put in prison and then put to death.

In the case of Herod Antipas's birthday—and it should be noted that Herod was a Jew, not pagan—the implied criticism is that he made a rash promise and bowed to social pressure (Matt. 14:9), which together led him to have John the Baptist executed. Neither of these is a criticism of birthdays but of rash oaths and bowing to peer pressure.

The mere mention of birthdays in these two texts does not allow one to infer that birthdays are being implicitly criticized. Good Bible interpretation does not permit taking a passage where something unpleasant is mentioned, finding a second element in the text, and from that alone inferring that the second element is being criticized.[9] This is the case especially when one has a very limited number of samples from which to draw. No firm conclusions can be drawn from a sampling of only two instances, as is the case here.

What about the other practices the Watchtower condemns? Is a practice or ritual necessarily displeasing to God if its roots can be traced back to paganism? No. Circumcision is a classic, biblical instance of this. Circumcision was a custom of pagan origin.

---

[9] Using the same logic, one could just as easily conclude that kings or executions or eating and drinking or celebrations of all kinds—including religious ones—are being implicitly criticized.

In Egypt (Jer. 9:25–26; Josh. 5:4–9) and among Semitic peoples generally, circumcision seems to have been practiced in antiquity. A relief in the Sixth Dynasty tomb of Ti (c. 2300 B.C.) at Saqqarah in Egypt depicts the operation of circumcision on 13-year-old youths.[10]

The third millennium before Christ, and more specifically 2300 B.C., was before Abraham, who lived in the early second millennium, thus, before he was given the covenant of circumcision by God in Genesis 17. Yet the fact that circumcision is of pagan origin did not prevent God from using it as a sign of his covenant with the people of Israel.

Further, Jehovah's Witnesses themselves have adopted things originally used by pagans. Wedding rings, marriage vows, white veils, and bridal bouquets are all of pagan origin, but you will likely find all of these at any Witness wedding. Even if some custom has a tainted past, so long as it is not *intrinsically* immoral it can be "baptized" and offered to God in spirit and truth.

The Watchtower's aversion to paganism is understandable, but it overlooks the fact that paganism is not *totally* wrong. There *are* elements of truth in paganism.[11] What makes paganism problematic is that those elements are obscured by sin and a flawed understanding of the nature of human existence. But when the elements of truth are distilled out of their pagan context and properly seen in the light of God's revelation, they are no longer problematic, as God is ultimately the source of all truth.

Even in secular matters, a Witness does not seem to realize how much of our modern culture is in some way connected with extinct pagan religion. If the Witness at your door is wearing Nike shoes, for instance, you might point out that Nike is the Greek goddess of victory. If the true God commanded that our lives be free from any and all references to paganism, the Witness would not only need to throw away his shoes, he would also have to rename the days of the week, months of the year, and even the planets of the solar system—as well as throw away his wedding

---

[10] *Wycliff Bible Encyclopedia* (Chicago: Moody Press, 1975), 1:354.

[11] For example, pagans commonly believe in the creation of the world, a supernatural dimension to the universe, and a moral code.

ring. Fortunately, God does not ask Christians to live in such scrupulosity.

Easter

What of the claim that Easter is of pagan origin because of its name and date of celebration? First of all, this objection could be only made by people who speak English or German. These seem to be the only languages of Christian countries where the Jewish name of Passover, *Pesach,* has not been retained to refer to the celebration of Christ's Resurrection. In Spain it is called *Pasca,* in Russia *Pashka,* in Italy *Pasqua,* in Greece *Pascha,* in France *Paque,*[12] but it is called *Ostern* in Germany and *Easter* in English-speaking countries. The feast of the Resurrection of Christ was well established, however, before the term *Easter* was given to it in the eighth century. The word "probably derives from *Eostur,* the Norse word for the Spring season, and not from *Eostre,* the name of an Anglo-Saxon goddess."[13]

It is equally absurd to claim that the term "Easter" was derived from the name of the goddess Ishtar merely because there is a similarity in the pronunciation of the two words. Ishtar was an Akkadian deity, and the Akkadian language had almost no influence on the development of the English language, whose primary sources are Germanic and Romance languages, not Hamitic-Semitic ones such as Akkadian.

Easter is celebrated on the first Sunday following the first full moon after the vernal (spring) equinox. This formula has nothing to do with paganism though. Since Christ was raised on a Sunday, the Church has chosen to set aside this day to celebrate the Resurrection. In the early Church, some objected to Sunday as the fixed day for the annual celebration. They wanted it to be linked to whatever day of the week 14 Nisan fell upon—14 Nisan was

---

[12] See *The Encyclopedia of Religion* (New York: Macmillan, 1987), 71, quoted in Ralph Woodrow, *Easter, Is It Pagan?* (Riverside, California: Ralph Woodrow Evangelistic Association, 1996), 19.

[13] Ibid., 2.

Passover in the Jewish calendar (and the actual day on which Jesus died).[14] Passover was celebrated on the first full moon on or after the spring equinox. Since Christ rose on the Sunday following the celebration of the Jewish Passover, the Church celebrates Easter on that day each year. The fact that Passover happens to take place in spring has nothing to do with perpetuating the worship of an Akkadian fertility goddess.

It is odd that the Watchtower will endorse the celebration of its Memorial of the Lord each year but not call to mind and rejoice in what happened three days later. It is only natural to recall and celebrate the day that Christ rose, which is why the first Christians adopted the practice!

Christmas

Is Christmas a pagan celebration merely because it is celebrated at the same time of the year as ancient pagan feasts honoring a sun god? If so, then one could just as easily argue that the Watchtower Theocratic Ministry School and Service Meetings are of pagan origin, since they are often held on Thursday—the day of the week named after the pagan deity Thor. Such a conclusion, obviously, would be silly. Nonetheless, the Watchtower seeks to convince the world that to win the favor of pagans, the early "apostate Church" established Christmas at the time of the pagan feast of *Sol Invictus*. This feast of "the unconquerable sun"—celebrated at the time of the winter solstice—was when the sun began to return to the northern skies and the days grew longer. It was essentially a celebration of the return of sunlight.

While one frequently encounters *assertions* that Christmas was timed to coincide with the celebration of *Sol Invictus*, these never seem to be backed up by *evidence*. In particular, they are never backed up by quotations from the early Christians saying, "We

---

[14] It should be noted that the standard Jewish calendar at the time of the Crucifixion was based on a mixed lunar-solar cycle and that 14 Nisan fell on a different day each year.

decided to time this celebration to coincide with *Sol Invictus*, and this is why . . ." If the early Church had deliberately decided to time the celebrations to coincide, this ought to be reflected in its writings, but it isn't. Witnesses never produce quotes from early Christians saying that Christmas was timed to coincide with a pagan festival. That is sheer speculation.

But let's suppose for a minute that there is evidence for such an idea. What message would be communicated by holding a Christian celebration on the same day as a prior pagan one? Would it be an endorsement of paganism? Hardly! Instead of trying to woo the pagans, the early Church's taking the sun god's feast day would have been *supplanting* it with a celebration of the birth of the true God. Ancient pagans would not consider it a compliment to their sun god that his birthday party had been replaced by one for the true "light of the world" (John 9:5; RSV:CE) and "sun of righteousness" (Mal. 4:2), Jesus Christ. In modern terms, this would be like taking the birthday of William J. Simmons, the founder of the modern Ku Klux Klan, and celebrating Martin Luther King Jr.'s accomplishments against racism on that day. This kind of triumphing over defeated paganism is something that the Church has often done down through the centuries. For example, in the middle of St. Peter's square in the Vatican is an enormous Egyptian obelisk that was erected by the emperor Caligula. The Church decided to let it remain, but with a cross placed atop it, saying in effect, "We win."

Lastly, should the celebration of Christmas be abolished because it is not mentioned in the Bible? To object to this holiday on these grounds involves having an extremely legalistic mind-set that presumes one cannot do anything unless there are explicit examples of it in Scripture. If this line of reasoning were followed consistently, it would prevent people from eating tomatoes, attending college, fishing with anything but a net, using microwave ovens, and even attending Kingdom Hall meetings on Sundays, since these are not expressly mandated in the Bible. Not only does this mind-set slip into scrupulosity; it is also an argument from silence, which is inherently problematic. Just because the celebration of Christmas is not explicitly mentioned in the Bible, one cannot assume that it is prohibited. If anything, the reverse is the case—all things are lawful for us, as Paul says in 1 Corinthians 6:12, as long as they are not prohibited.

The Jews of the Old Testament would celebrate festivals, new moons, sabbaths, and various other feasts throughout the year, recalling the great things that God had done for them. The origin of some of these, such as Hanukkah, cannot be found in the *New World Translation*, but Jesus himself observed this feast (John 10:22). Another feast day he observed was that of the Passover, calling to mind the saving work of God in bringing Israel out of the bondage of Egypt (Luke 22:15).

Even the exchange of gifts on holidays is countenanced in Scripture. Thus we read of the feast of Purim:

> Mordecai proceeded to write these things and send written documents to all the Jews . . . to impose upon them the obligation to be regularly holding the fourteenth day of the month A'dar and the fifteenth day of it in each and every year, according to the days on which the Jews had rested from their enemies and the month that was changed for them from grief to rejoicing and from mourning to a good day, to hold them as days of banqueting and rejoicing and sending of portions to one another and of gifts to the poor people. (Esther 9:20–22)

Like Passover and the feast of Purim, Christmas is a celebration that commemorates God's victory over sin, when he delivered man from the bondage of the evil one. Easter is the commemoration of his victory over death. Surely such occasions are worthy of celebration!

15

Can You Trust the
New World Translation?

The New World Translation *was prepared by anointed witnesses of Je-hovah, who transmitted his thoughts and declarations as accurately as possi-ble. These men have chosen to remain anonymous, since they did not seek prominence, and God's word should stand on its merits. The* NWT *is an accurate, largely literal translation from the original languages. It is not a loose paraphrase in which the authors add ideas that they believe will be helpful.*[1]

From 1950 to 1961, the Watchtower created the *New World Translation of the Holy Scriptures* in several parts, beginning with the New Testament. It is considered by Witnesses to be the only reliable modern translation, though they may use other ones for the purpose of discussion. The *NWT* was produced by an anony-mous committee, which altered passages that had proved to be problematic for earlier Witnesses. Ostensibly, it is an anonymous work so that only Jehovah would get the glory for it, instead of men. But, the Watchtower admits, "since the translators have cho-sen to remain anonymous, the question here cannot be answered in terms of their educational background."[2]

It has been learned, however, that Nathan Knorr, Frederick Franz, Albert Schroeder, Milton Henschel, and George Gangas

---

[1] *Reasoning from the Scriptures* (Brooklyn: Watchtower Bible and Tract Soci-ety of New York, 1985), 276–77.

[2] Ibid., 277.

produced the text,[3] which, understandably, is used by no other sect. One must wonder why their educational backgrounds were not made public. As it turns out, the extent of the scholarly credentials possessed by the Translation Committee was that *one* of its members, Frederick Franz, had studied non-biblical Greek for two years at the University of Cincinnati and was allegedly self-taught in Hebrew. Frederick Franz later admitted before a court that he could neither read nor speak Hebrew.

The remaining committee members had no formal training in any biblical language. There were no degrees in Greek, Hebrew, or Aramaic among the five of them, and this lack of formal education can be seen, for example, in their attempt to translate I Corinthians 5:1, which in the NWT reads: "Actually fornication is reported among YOU, and such fornication as is not even among the nations, that a wife a certain [man] has of [his] father."

Biblical scholar H. H. Rowley said that the NWT "reminds one of nothing so much as a schoolboy's first painful beginnings in translating Latin into English . . . and instead of showing the reverence for the Bible which the translators profess, it is an insult to the word of God."[4]

Listed below are some examples of how the text of the NWT is deliberately mistranslated to fit Watchtower belief. Though many more examples could be given,[5] here are some key verses the Watchtower has deliberately mistranslated in order to fit its doctrines:

1. John 1:1—To undermine the divinity of Christ in John 1:1, the NWT reads, "the word was *a* god" (emphasis added). This translation is wrong. In order to explain its proper translation, one

---

[3] Raymond Franz, *Crisis of Conscience* (Atlanta: Commentary Press, 1983), 50 n. 15; see also William I. Cetnar, *Questions for JWs Who Love the Truth* (self-published, 1983), 68.

[4] "So Many Versions?" *Expository Times*, 65 (1953–1954), 103.

[5] See the article "65 questions every Jehovah's Witness should be asked using the NWT" at *www.webshowplace.com/question*.

needs to get a bit technical. Witnesses argue that since the Greek phrase in question in John 1:1 (*theos ēn ho logos*) does not use the definite article before the word *god* (in which case it would read *ho theos ēn ho logos*), it must refer to "*a god.*" Witnesses argue that in the Greek, if you have a singular noun appearing without the article *the* before the verb, the indefinite article *a* is inferred. Thus, the translation becomes "a god" rather than "God." If this were true, however, the Watchtower would run into significant difficulties.

Daniel B. Wallace is worth quoting at length regarding this issue:

> If *theos*[6] were indefinite, we would translate it "a god" (as done in the *New World Translation* [NWT]). If so, then the theological implication would be some form of polytheism, perhaps suggesting that the Word was merely a secondary god in a pantheon of deities.
>
> The grammatical argument that the PN [predicate nominative] here is indefinite is weak. Often, those who argue for such a view (in particular, the translators of the NWT) do so on the sole basis that the term is anarthrous [without the article]. Yet they are inconsistent, as R. H. Countess pointed out:
>
> "In the New Testament there are 282 occurrences of the anarthrous *theos*. At sixteen places NWT has either a god, god, gods, or godly. Sixteen out of 282 means that the translators were faithful to *their* translation principle only six percent of the time. . . .
>
> "The first section of John—1:1–18—furnishes a lucid example of NWT arbitrary dogmatism. *Theos* occurs eight times—verses 1, 2, 6, 12, 13, 18—and has the article only twice—verses 1, 2. Yet NWT six times translated 'God,' once 'a god,' and once 'the god.' "
>
> If we expand the discussion to other anarthrous terms in the Johannine Prologue, we notice other inconsistencies in the NWT: It is interesting that the *New World Translation* renders *theos* as "a god" on the simplistic grounds that it lacks the article. This is

---

[6] Wallace uses the Greek alphabet to represent Greek words. We have put them in the English alphabet for benefit of those unfamiliar with the Greek alphabet. Thus θεὸς becomes *theos*.

surely an insufficient basis. Following the "anarthrous = indefinite" principle would mean that *archē* should be "a beginning" (1:1, 2), *zōē* should be "a life" (1:4), *para theou* should be "from a god" (1:6), *Joannēs* should be "a John" (1:6), *theon*[7] should be "a god" (1:18), etc. Yet none of these other anarthrous nouns is rendered with an indefinite article. One can only suspect strong theological bias in such a translation.[8]

The Watchtower uses the work of Greek scholar Julius Mantey to support its rendering of John 1:1 (KIT). When Mantey discovered what had been taken from his book *A Manual Grammar of the Greek New Testament*, he wrote to the Watchtower Bible and Tract Society:

> You quoted me out of context. . . . [I]t is neither scholarly nor reasonable to translate John 1:1 "The Word was a god." Word order has made obsolete and incorrect such a rendering. Your quotation of Colwell's rule [of Greek grammar] is inadequate because it quotes only part of his findings. You did not quote this strong assertion: "A predicate nominative which precedes the verb cannot be translated as an indefinite or a 'qualitative' noun solely because of the absence of the article." Colwell and Harner have stated that *theos* in John 1:1 is not indefinite and should not be translated as "a god." Watchtower writers appear to be the only ones advocating such a translation now. The evidence appears to be 99% against them.[9]

Mantey went on to request a public apology and retraction from the Watchtower, mentioning the threat of a lawsuit.

In addition to quoting Greek scholars out of context, the Watchtower gives eight translations that support its rendering of John 1:1. The first is *The New Testament, in an Improved Version, Upon the Basis of Archbishop Newcombe's New Translation*. This version

---

[7] This is the same word as *theos*, above. Here it ends with an *-n* rather than an *-s* because in 1:18 it is a direct object and so is placed in the accusative case.

[8] *Greek Grammar Beyond the Basics: An Exegetical Syntax of the New Testament* (Grand Rapids: Zondervan, 1996), 266–67.

[9] Letter dated July 11, 1974.

rendered John 1:1 as "the word was God" until the Unitarians (who deny the divinity of Christ) altered the text.

The next translation used by the Watchtower as supporting evidence is the *Monotessaron; or The Gospel History, According to the Four Evangelists*, by John S. Thompson.[10] Thompson, who was a Unitarian minister with universalist beliefs, published this work himself. It is an obscure work done by a man who had been Calvinist, then Arminian, Restorationist, Arian Restorationist, and then Unitarian and admitted having had experiences with spirit beings who instructed him in his translation. In the *American Quarterly Review* of September 1830, Thompson said, "I shall rejoice in having been the happy instrument, in the hand of God, of having done fourfold as much for mankind, as all the professed commentators of the last fifteen centuries!"[11]

Translation number three is the *Emphatic Diaglott*, by Benjamin Wilson (1864). Wilson taught himself Greek, and he was a Christadelphian—another sect that denies the divinity of Christ. Wilson's diaglott includes the Greek New Testament, an interlinear English translation, and an English translation in the margin. Within the interlinear translation, Wilson renders the phrase in John 1:1 as "a god," but in his margin translation, he renders it as "God."

The fourth version is *The Bible—An American Translation*.[12] This is a respectable translation, but it merely says, "The Word was divine." This rendering does not lend support to the NWT, since even Catholics would agree with the statement.

The fifth translation offered is the 1950 edition of the *New World*

---

[10] John S. Thompson, *Monotessaron; or The Gospel History, According to the Four Evangelists* (Baltimore: publisher anonymous, 1829).

[11] John S. Thompson, *The American Quarterly Review*, 8 (September 1830): 227–45, quoted in Leonard and Marjorie Chretien, *Witnesses of Jehovah* (Eugene, Oregon: Harvest House Publishers, 1988), 169.

[12] J. M. P. Smith and E. J. Goodspeed, *The Bible—An American Translation* (Chicago: University of Chicago, 1935).

Translation of the Christian Greek Scriptures. Here the Watchtower uses its own translation for support.

The last three are German translations from 1975, 1978, and 1979. The Watchtower seemingly hopes that no one will find these translations or translate the German. The three read as follows:

Shultz' translation: "*und ein Gott (oder: Gott von Art) war das Wort.*"
In English: "and one [a] God (or: God of a kind) was the Word."

Schneider's translation: "*und Göttlicher Art war der Logos.*"
In English: "and a form of divinity was the Logos."

Becker's translation: "*und ein Gott war der Logos.*"
In English: "and one [a] God was the Logos." [13]

So, of the eight translations that supposedly lend credence to the Watchtower rendering of John 1:1, one was changed to fit theological presuppositions of Unitarians; the second was claimed to have been written with the assistance of spirit beings; the third is an interlinear at odds with the author's own translation—an author who taught himself Greek and beforehand had denied the divinity of Christ; the fourth uses a different wording from that of the Watchtower translation; the fifth is the Watchtower's own translation; and the last three are German texts that are also worded differently from the NWT. The Watchtower appears to be desperate for support, since none can be found.

A translator who used to be cited by the Watchtower was Johannes Greber. Despite acknowledging in 1956 that Greber used spirits to help him translate the New Testament,[14] the Watchtower used his translation as supporting evidence for decades. In the "Questions from Readers" column, *The Watchtower* was asked why Greber was no longer used for support. *The Watchtower* responded:

---

[13] Translation provided by The Language Connection, Carlsbad, California. In the above translations "[a]" is an alternate translation for "one."

[14] *The Watchtower*, 15 February 1956, 110–11.

But as indicated in a foreword to the 1980 edition of *The New Testament* by Johannes Greber, this translator relied on "God's Spirit World" to clarify for him how he should translate difficult passages. It is stated: "His wife, a medium of God's Spiritworld was often instrumental in conveying the correct answers from God's Messengers to Pastor Greber." *The Watchtower* has deemed it improper to make use of a translation that has such a close rapport with spiritism. [15]

In contrast to those translations used by the Watchtower, there are numerous translations that render John 1:1 as "the Word was God." They include the *King James Version*, the *New King James Version*, the *Jerusalem Bible*, the *New American Bible*, the *Revised Standard Version*, the *Douay Rheims Version*, the *American Standard Version*, the *New International Version*, the *New American Standard Bible*, and countless others, all of which are mainstream translations recognized as valid and reputable within the scholarly community. Ironically, even *The Emphatic Diaglott*, which has been republished by the Watchtower, renders John 1:1 as "the Word was God."

2. Colossians 1:16–17—Referring to Jesus, these verses state that "by means of him all things were created. . . . He is before all things." It has been changed in the NWT to "by means of him all [other] things were created. . . . He is before all [other] things." If the text of this passage and surrounding verses were translated in accordance with what the Greek text actually says, it would state several times that Jesus created all things. However, the Watchtower cannot afford to say that anyone but Jehovah created all things, since "he that constructed all things is God" (Heb. 3:4). So *other* was inserted four times into these two verses, thus making the passage assert something other than what it actually says. (There is a big difference between saying that Jesus created *all* things and saying that he created all *other* things. The former makes him God; the latter implies that he was created.) Without

---

[15] *The Watchtower*, 1 April 1983, 31.

the inserted words, the text reads: "by means of him all things were created in the heavens and the earth, the things visible and the things invisible. . . . All things have been created through him and for him. Also, he is before all things and by means of him all things were made to exist." When the text is left alone, it tells a different story from that of the Watchtower.

3. John 8:58—When correctly translated, this verse quotes Jesus as saying, "before Abraham came to be, I AM" (NAB), but the NWT mistranslates this verse to read, "Before Abraham came into existence, I have been." This change is an attempt to cover up Jesus' use of the title "I AM" used by God in Exodus 3:14 when he appears to Moses in the burning bush. In Greek, "I AM" is *egō eimi*, and this is what appears at Exodus 3:14 in the Septuagint. Strangely, the NWT translates the Greek words *egō eimi* as "I am" each time they appear in John,[16] *except* in John 8:58, where they are rendered "I have been." The Watchtower is not being consistent in its translation principles, and it is not mere coincidence that the one place it breaks from those principles is in a verse where Jesus most clearly asserts his divinity.

To justify this unique rendering of John 8:58, the Watchtower argues that Jesus was referring to his age, not his title.[17] But Jesus was not using the expression merely to explain that he came before Abraham. By using the phrase God used at the burning bush, he was asserting his eternal nature. Both times when God used the phrase "I AM" in Exodus, it expressed an identity. "I AM" is a title that expresses the eternal nature of God—not that he will be or has been but that he *is*, as the one who is eternally present, the very source of being. That is his nature, so that is his title.

Even if the Watchtower's translation as "I have been" were accurate, it would still leave the Witnesses with a difficult problem. It still remains that in Exodus 3:14 in the Septuagint (the standard Greek translation of the Old Testament) God is depicted as apply-

---

[16] John 6:35, 6:41, 8:24, 13:19, 15:5, etc.

[17] *Reasoning from the Scriptures*, 418.

ing the same Greek phrase to himself—*egō eimi*—that Jesus did in John 8:58, making the connection between the two passages even more ambiguous, the NWT renders the divine Name "I AM" in Exodus 3:14 as "I shall prove to be what I shall prove to be." Finally, we should note that apart from the understanding that Jesus was applying the divine name to himself, the verses around John 8:58 would make no sense, since the crowd attempted to stone him for blasphemy, there being no punishment of stoning for those who say, "I have been."

4. Hebrews 1:6 and similar verses—The 1953, 1960, 1961, and 1970 editions of the NWT as well as the Watchtower's KIT say in various passages that Jesus is to be worshiped, but the Watchtower changed the NWT in 1971 so that the new version would not contradict its doctrine. With this edition, the Greek word for worship (*proskuneō*) is rendered as "do obeisance" every time it is applied to Jesus,[18] but as "worship" when in reference to Jehovah.[19] While the word *proskuneō* can legitimately be translated "to do obeisance," once again we see the Watchtower's systematic editing out of things attributed to the Son that it teaches can only be attributed to the Father.

5. Matthew 26:26, Mark 14:22, Luke 22:19—Since the Watchtower denies the two-thousand-year-old Catholic teaching on the Real Presence of Jesus in the Eucharist, it has taken the liberty to change our Lord's words to "This *means* my body" in the institution narratives of the synoptic Gospels, even though the Greek is very clear. Jesus says, "This *is* my body" (Greek, *Touto estin to sōma mou*; literally, "This is the body of me"). *Estin* is the third person singular form of the present tense verb *to be*. It means *is*.

6. Romans 10:9, 1 Corinthians 12:3, Philippians 2:11, Revelation 22:21—The NWT translates the Greek word *Lord* (*kurios*) as

---

[18] Matt. 8:2, 9:18, 14:33, 15:25, 17, 28:9; Mark 5:6, 15:19; Luke 24:52; John 9:38; Heb. 1:6, etc.

[19] John 4:20; Rev. 5:14, 7:11, 11:16, 19:4, etc.

"Jehovah" throughout the New Testament,[20] despite the fact that the word *Jehovah* is *never* used by *any* New Testament author. If the Watchtower consistently translated *kurios* as "Jehovah," Jesus would be "Jehovah" in these passages.

7. Matthew 25:46—What actually reads "eternal punishment" (*kolasin aiōnion*) in Matthew 25:46 is now rendered as "everlasting cutting-off." Translating the Greek *kolasis*[21] as "cutting-off" is out of the question. No lexicon gives this as a translation for this noun. *Reasoning from the Scriptures* offers this argument:

> A footnote states "*Kolasin* . . . is derived from *kolazoō* which signifies, 1. *To cut off;* as lopping off branches of trees, to prune. 2. *To restrain, to repress . . .* 3. *To chastise, to punish.* To cut off an individual from life, or society, or even restrain, is esteemed as *punishment.*"[22]

But the book does not even mention the source of this footnote, which likely means that it is from another Watchtower publication. But of more significance is the Watchtower's attempt to avoid explaining the definition of one word by defining a similar word.

The word Scripture uses when describing hell is not *kolazoō*, which is a verb, but *kolasis*, a noun that means "chastisement," "punishment," "severe punishments which precede execution," and "torments which martyrs had to endure."[23] The root word does have the multiple meanings the Watchtower provides, but the definition of a root word is not the same as the definition of a word derived from it. The failure to realize this is called the etymological fallacy. For example, the original meaning of *anathema* was "something to be set among the holy things." When Paul

---

[20] Matt. 3:3, Luke 2:9, John 1:23, Acts 21:14, Rom. 12:19, Col. 1:10, 1 Thess. 5:2, 1 Pet. 1:25, Rev. 4:8, etc.

[21] *Kolasis* is the dictionary form of the word *kolasin*, which has been inflected in Matt. 25:46 to indicate its grammatical role in the text.

[22] *Reasoning from the Scriptures*, 171.

[23] Kittel, *Theological Dictionary of the New Testament* (Grand Rapids: Eerdmans, 1965), 3:816.

says, "let him be *anathema*" in Galatians 1:8, he clearly does not have this in mind. (A more modern example of this dynamic is the word "nice," which is derived from a French word meaning "silly" or "foolish.") David Hill of the University of Sheffield writes,

> Etymology is no sure guide to the semantic value of words in their current usage. . . . Such value has to be determined from the current usage itself and not from derivation. The etymology of a word . . . is not a statement about its meaning, but about its history, and the historical past of a word is not a reliable guide to its present meaning.[24]

8. Philippians 1:23—In this verse, which also deals with what happens at death, the NWT has Paul stating, "but what I do desire is *the releasing and the being with Christ*" as opposed to, "My desire is *to depart and be with Christ*" (RSV:CE; emphasis added). In this passage, St. Paul is speaking about his death. He longs to be with the Lord, though he realizes it is better for the sake of the Church that he remain in the flesh for the time being. Since the Watchtower denies that Paul would be conscious after his death, the NWT appendix clarifies that "the releasing" can't refer to Paul's death[25] but must refer to Christ's return. After all, the Witnesses reason, the apostle can't mean that "at his death he would be changed into spirit and would be with Christ forever." But that is exactly what Paul has said.

This maneuver on the part of the Watchtower is a key example of the translators' willingness to distort Scripture to fit the teaching. The key words in the Greek text are *analusai* and *einai*. These are both infinitives and would normally be translated in English with infinitives—"to depart" and "to be."

---

[24] *Greek Words and Hebrew Meanings* (Cambridge: University Press, 1967), 3. See also James Barr, *The Semantics of Biblical Language* (Oxford: Oxford University Press, 1961).

[25] Elsewhere, the NWT says that "releasing" does refer to Paul's death (see 2 Tim. 4:6).

9. Other verses showing Jesus' divinity—Since the New Testament is replete with evidence that Jesus is God, the Watchtower has had to patch up several other verses besides John 1:1. Listed below are four additional examples, given in pairs, with an accurate translation first, followed by the NWT version:

> [Of the Jewish race,] according to the flesh, is the Christ, who is God over all, blessed forever. (Rom. 9:5; RSV:CE)
> Christ [sprang] according to the flesh: God, who is over all [be] blessed forever (Rom. 9:5; NWT)

> [A]dorn the doctrine of God our Savior. . . . the appearing of the glory of our great God and Savior Jesus Christ. (Titus 2:10, 13; RSV:CE)
> [A]dorn the teaching of our Savior, God, in all things. . . . glorious manifestation of the great God and of [the] Savior of us, Christ Jesus. (Titus 2:10, 13; NWT)

> "Thy throne, O God, is forever and ever." (Heb. 1:8; RSV:CE)
> "God is your throne forever and ever." (Heb. 1:8; NWT)

> [O]ur God and Savior Jesus Christ. (2 Pet. 1:1; RSV:CE)
> [O]ur God and [the] Savior Jesus Christ. (2 Pet. 1:1; NWT)

Two of these verses require further discussion. In Titus 2:13 we read of "our great God and Savior, Jesus Christ." The Greek for this is *tou megalou theou kai sōtēros hēmōn Iēsou Christou*. In 2 Peter 1:1, an almost identical phrase appears. It speaks of "our God and Savior Jesus Christ," the Greek for which is *tou theou hēmōn kai sōtēros Iēsou Christou*. Both of these phrases are subject to a principle of Greek syntax known as "Granville Sharp's Rule," after the man who identified it. With some simplification, Sharp's rule is essentially this: "When you have two nouns, which are not proper names (such as Cephas, or Paul, or Timothy), which are describing a person, and the two nouns are connected by the word 'and,' and the first noun has the article *the* while the second does not, both nouns are referring to the same person."[26]

---

[26] "Granville Sharp's Rule," *www.caic.org.au/jws/granvill.htm*. Cult Awareness and Information Centre (*www.caic.org.au*).

There are eighty such constructions in the New Testament, and there are no exceptions to the rule. So when 2 Peter 1:11, 2:20 and 3:18 say, "Lord and Savior Jesus Christ," it is clear from the rules of Greek syntax that Jesus is both Lord and Savior. Both nouns refer to the same person. The same is true with 2 Peter 1:1 and Titus 2:13 when they refer to "God and Savior Jesus Christ." The syntax is identical; the only differences between 2 Peter 1:1 and 1:11 in the Greek are the words *Lord* and *God*.[27] The Watchtower has no grounds on which to base its translation "God and [the] Savior Jesus Christ"—implying that they are two different persons.[28]

---

[27] "*[T]ou theou* [God] *hēmōn kai sōtēros Iēsou Christou*" (2 Pet. 1:1) and "*tou kuriou* [Lord] *hēmōn kai sōtēros Iēsou Christou*" (2 Pet. 1:11).

[28] For a full discussion of Granville Sharp's Rule and how it applies to these passages, see Wallace, *Greek Grammar Beyond the Basics*, 270–90.

16

Can You Trust
Watchtower Predictions?

The Watchtower is God's reliable mouthpiece and prophet to the nations.[1]
*It is "the mouthpiece of Jehovah God" and the "one channel that the Lord
is using during the last days of this system of things."*[2] *Jesus inspected the
different churches and religious teachings of the world in 1918, and he found
one faithful servant that was distributing spiritual food in due season. This
was the Watchtower.*

The Watchtower makes high claims for itself. It claims the
exclusive right to speak for God in the present day, and its pro-
nouncements have a profound impact on the lives of its adherents.
As we will see, Witnesses have been actively encouraged by the
Watchtower to make important life decisions—such as whether
to get married, have children, go to college, or pick a particular
career—based on the organization's statements on how close Armageddon is. Many Witnesses have followed the Watchtower's di-
rections in determining the course of their lives. Based on various
Watchtower predictions of the imminent arrival of Armageddon,

---

[1] *The Watchtower*, 15 January 1959, 40–41; 1 April 1972, 197; 1 October
1982, 26–27; *The Nations Shall Know That I am Jehovah—How?* (Brooklyn:
Watchtower Bible and Tract Society of New York, 1971), 58–59, 70–71; *Holy
Spirit—The Force Behind the Coming New Order!* (Brooklyn: Watchtower Bible
and Tract Society of New York, 1976), 148.

[2] *Jehovah's Witnesses: Proclaimers of God's Kingdom* (Brooklyn: Watchtower
Bible and Tract Society of New York, 1993), 626.

many Witnesses have chosen not to get married and have children or not to go to college or to take low-paying, part-time jobs so that they could spend more of their time evangelizing.

These same Witnesses have felt disappointed, cheated, betrayed, and ashamed when the dates predicted for the beginning of Armageddon have come and gone. The Watchtower has led its readers to expect Armageddon to occur in 1914,[3] 1918,[4] 1925,[5] during World War II,[6] in 1975,[7] and before the last members of the "generation of 1914" died.[8] An instructive list of Watchtower reversals was published in 1990.[9]

Let us look at some of the things the Watchtower has predicted, bearing in mind the pastoral damage these predictions did to the lives of its followers:

> 1889—"[T]he 'battle of the great day of God almighty' (Rev. 16:14), which will end in A.D. 1914 with the complete overthrow of earth's present rulership, is already commenced."[10]
>
> 1891—"[W]ith the end of A.D. 1914, what God calls Babylon, and what men call Christendom, will have passed away, as already shown from prophecy."[11]

---

[3] Charles Taze Russell, *Studies in the Scriptures* (Brooklyn: International Bible Students Association, 1911), 2:101; *Watchtower Reprints*, 1355 (*Zion's Watch Tower*, 15 January 1892, 22).

[4] *Studies in the Scriptures* (Brooklyn: People's Pulpit Association, 1917), 7:62, 485.

[5] *Millions Now Living Will Never Die* (Brooklyn: Watchtower Bible and Tract Society of New York, 1920), 89–90; *The Watchtower*, 15 July 1924, 211.

[6] *The Watchtower*, 15 September 1941, 288.

[7] *Our Kingdom Ministry*, June 1969, 3; *Awake!*, 8 October 1968.

[8] *You Can Live Forever in Paradise on Earth* (Brooklyn: Watchtower Bible and Tract Society of New York, 1982), 154; *Awake!*, 8 October 1995, 4.

[9] David Reed, ed., *Index of Watchtower Errors* (Grand Rapids: Baker Book House, 1990).

[10] *Studies in the Scriptures*, (*The Time Is at Hand*) (Brooklyn: International Bible Students Association, 1889), 2:101.

[11] Charles Taze Russell, *Studies in the Scriptures* (Brooklyn: Watchtower Bible and Tract Society, 1891), 3:153.

1894—"The end of 1914 is not the date for the *beginning*, but for the *end* of the time of trouble."[12]

1897—"Our Lord is now present, since October 1874 A.D., according to the testimony of the prophets."[13]

1914—"The present great war in Europe is the beginning of the Armageddon of the Scriptures (Rev. 16:16–20). It will eventuate in the complete overthrow of all the systems of error which have so long oppressed the people of God and deluded the world."[14]

1916—"The six great 1000 year days beginning with Adam are ended, and that the great 7th day, the 1000 years of Christ's reign began in 1873."[15]

1917—"Scriptures . . . prove that the Lord's Second Advent occurred in the fall of 1874."[16]

1918—God will destroy "churches wholesale and the church members by millions."[17] "Even the republics will disappear in the fall of 1920."[18]

1918—"Therefore, we may confidently expect that 1925 will mark the return of Abraham, Isaac, Jacob, and the faithful prophets of old . . . to the condition of human perfection."[19]

1922—"The date 1925 is even more distinctly indicated by the Scriptures [than 1914] because it is fixed by the law God gave to Israel."[20]

1923—"Our thought is, that 1925 is definitely settled by the Scriptures, marking the end of the typical jubilees. . . . As to Noah, the Christian now has much more upon which to base his faith than Noah had upon which to base his faith in a coming deluge."[21]

---

[12] *Watchtower Reprints*, 1677 (*Zion's Watch Tower*, 15 July 1894, 226; italics in original).

[13] Charles Taze Russell, *Studies in the Scriptures* (Brooklyn: Watchtower Bible and Tract Society, 1923), 4:621.

[14] *Pastor Russell's Sermons* (Brooklyn: People's Pulpit Association, 1917), 676.

[15] *The Time Is at Hand*, 1923 ed., foreword.

[16] *The Finished Mystery*, 1918 ed., 68.

[17] Ibid., 485, 513.

[18] Ibid., 258.

[19] *Millions Now Living Will Never Die*, 89.

[20] *The Watchtower*, 1 September 1922, 262.

[21] Ibid., 1 April 1923, 106.

1924—"The year 1925 is a date definitively and clearly marked in the Scriptures, even more clearly than that of 1914."[22]

1924—"We should, therefore, expect shortly after 1925 to see the awakening of Abel, Enoch, Noah, Abraham, Isaac, Jacob, Melchisedec, Job, Moses, Samuel, David, Isaiah, Jeremiah, Ezekiel, Daniel, John the Baptist, and others mentioned in the eleventh chapter of Hebrews."[23]

1925—"The year of 1925 is here. With great expectation Christians have looked forward to this year . . . Christians should not be so deeply concerned about what may *transpire* during this year that they would fail to joyfully *do* what the Lord would have them do."[24]

1926—"Some anticipated that the work would end in 1925, but the Lord did not state so."[25]

1931—"There was a measure of disappointment on the part of Jehovah's faithful ones on earth concerning the dates 1914, 1918, and 1925 . . . and they also learned to quit fixing dates for the future and predicting what would come to pass on a certain date."[26]

1938—Armageddon is so near that Witnesses should wait until it is over before they marry and raise children.[27]

1939—"The disaster of Armageddon is just ahead."[28]

1941—Since Armageddon is only months away,[29] a fictional Witness couple decides to defer plans of marriage until paradise on earth is established.[30]

1941—"Armageddon is surely near . . . soon . . . within a few years."[31]

---

[22] Ibid., 15 July 1924, 211.

[23] *The Way to Paradise* (Brooklyn: Watchtower Bible and Tract Society, 1924), 224.

[24] *The Watchtower*, 1 January 1925, 3; italics in original.

[25] Ibid., 1 August 1926, 232.

[26] *Vindication* (Brooklyn: Watchtower Bible and Tract Society, 1931), 1:388–89.

[27] *The Watchtower*, 1 November 1938, 323.

[28] J. F. Rutherford, *Salvation* (Brooklyn: Watchtower Bible and Tract Society of New York, 1939), 361.

[29] *The Watchtower*, 15 September 1941, 288.

[30] *Children* (Brooklyn: Watchtower Bible and Tract Society, 1941), 366.

[31] Ibid., 10.

1942—"The Lord Jesus has now come to the temple for judgment, and the remnant of the members of 'his body' yet on earth he has gathered into the temple condition of perfect unity with himself (Mal. 3:1–3), and hence those faithful men of old may be expected back from the dead any day now."[32]

1946—"Armageddon . . . should come sometime before 1972."[33]

1966—"According to this trustworthy Bible chronology, six thousand years from man's creation will end in 1975, and the seventh period of a thousand years of human history will begin in the fall of 1975 C.E. So six thousand years of man's existence on earth will soon be up, yes, within this generation."[34] (The implication is that Christ's millennial reign would begin that same year.)

1968—"What about all this talk concerning the year 1975? Lively discussions, some based on speculation, have burst into flame during recent months among serious students of the Bible. Their interest has been kindled by the belief that 1975 will mark the end of 6,000 years of human history since Adam's creation."[35]

1969—"Of course, there may be a tempting offer of higher education or of going into some field of work that promises material rewards. However, Jehovah God holds out to you young folks many marvelous privileges of service in his organization. Which will you decide to take up? In view of the short time left, a decision to pursue a career in this system of things is not only unwise but extremely dangerous."[36]

1974—In preparation for 1975, the year Armageddon would allegedly take place, many Witnesses quit jobs and sold their homes: "Reports are heard of brothers selling their homes and property and planning to finish out the rest of their days in this old system in the pioneer service. Certainly this is a fine way to spend the short time remaining before the wicked world's end."[37]

---

[32] *The New World* (Brooklyn: Watchtower Bible and Tract Society, 1942), 104.

[33] *They Have Found a Faith* (Brooklyn: Watchtower Bible and Tract Society, 1946), 44.

[34] *Life Everlasting—In Freedom of the Sons of God* (Brooklyn: Watchtower Bible and Tract Society of New York, 1966), 29.

[35] *The Watchtower*, 15 August 1968, 494.

[36] *Our Kingdom Ministry*, June 1969, 3.

[37] Ibid., May 1974, 3.

When the world failed to end in 1975, hundreds of thousands of Witnesses left the organization, marking the first time in the sect's history that overall membership significantly decreased. To attempt to explain the miscalculation, Watchtower President Frederick Franz said that the six-thousand-year chronology of the history of man began with the creation of Eve—not Adam, as was previously thought. But the Watchtower also stated that it was not known how much time passed between the creation of Adam and the creation of Eve. This "refinement" in teaching had the net result of buying the Watchtower more time in hopes of seeing its prediction fulfilled.

But its clock was ticking down. It had elsewhere promised that the millennium of the new paradise earth had to come before all of the "anointed class" from 1914 had died. (As was noted above, this truth was so central to Watchtower teaching that it was continuously affirmed in the masthead of *Awake!* magazine until 1995.) In 1968, the Watchtower wrote that "the youngest of 'this generation' [would be] nearly 70 years old today."[38] Thus, the members of the "generation of 1914" would be 100 years old at the turn of the millennium. Also in 1968, the Watchtower wrote:

> But there are people still living who were alive in 1914 and saw what was happening then and who were old enough that they still remember those events. This generation is getting up in years now. A great number of them has already passed away in death. Yet Jesus very pointedly said: "This generation will *by no means* pass away until all these things occur." Some of them will still be alive to see the end of this wicked system. This means that only a short time is left before the end comes! (Psalm 90:10 [89:10]) So now is the time to take urgent action if you do not want to be swept away with this wicked system.[39]

---

[38] *The Watchtower*, 8 October 1968, 13–14.

[39] *The Truth That Leads to Eternal Life* (Brooklyn: Watchtower Bible and Tract Society of New York, 1968), 95.

The reference to Psalm 90:10 indicates how long a generation is—between seventy and eighty years. Thus, the "generation of 1914" ended by 1994 at the latest. With this in mind, the Watchtower had to make an abrupt change in the masthead of *Awake!* What had once read, "This magazine builds confidence in the Creator's promise of a peaceful and secure new world before the generation that saw the events of 1914 passes away" (1991) was changed to "This magazine builds confidence in the Creator's promise of a peaceful and secure new world that is about to replace the present wicked, lawless system of things" (1999). Note that the reference to the generation of 1914 is missing.

Before most of its prophecies had failed, the Watchtower wrote, "The false prophets of our day are the financial, political and clerical prognosticators. They assume to foretell future events; but their dreams or guesses never come true. . . . Therefore they are false prophets; and the people should no longer trust them as safe guides."[40] The Watchtower also noted that other groups had "predicted the end of the world even announcing a specific date. . . . The 'end' did not come. They were guilty of false prophesying."[41] After its own predicted dates had come and gone, the Watchtower asserted that Witnesses do not claim to be inspired prophets,[42] but prior Watchtower publications did claim divine approval for their statements.[43]

The Watchtower has been honest enough in recent decades to admit having "missed the mark" on occasion, but rather than acknowledge its false prophecies, it claims that the organization had

---

[40] *The Watchtower*, 15 May 1930, 155–56.

[41] *Awake!*, 8 October 1968, 23.

[42] *Reasoning from the Scriptures* (Brooklyn: Watchtower Bible and Tract Society of New York, 1985) 136, 137.

[43] *The Watchtower*, 1 April 1972, 197; 1 October 1982, 27; *The Nations Shall Know That I Am Jehovah—How?* (Brooklyn: Watchtower Bible and Tract Society of New York, 1971), 58–59, 70–71; *Holy Spirit—The Force Behind the Coming New Order!* (Brooklyn: Watchtower Bible and Tract Society of New York, 1976), 148.

insufficient "light" (i.e., truth and understanding). Moreover, the organization is quick to point a finger at Christendom for what it considers to be Christendom's own failures:

> It is easy for the established churches of Christendom and other people to criticize Jehovah's Witnesses because their publications have, at times, stated that certain things could take place on certain dates. But is not such line of action in harmony with Christ's injunction to "keep on the watch"? (Mark 13:37) On the other hand, have Christendom's churches encouraged Christian watchfulness by teaching that the Kingdom is "the ruling of God in our hearts"? Have they not, rather, encouraged spiritual sluggishness by considering expectation of "the end" to be "meaningless" or "an insignificant myth"? Have apostates who claim that "the last days" began at Pentecost and cover the entire Christian Era promoted Christian alertness? Have they not, rather, induced spiritual sleepiness?[44]

What does this mean from the Watchtower's point of view? Well, it would seem that Witnesses want to appear eager to see God's will come to pass, while "apostate Christendom" folds its arms to rest, not expecting the return of Christ because it is not setting dates. Of course, refusing to set dates for the end of the world is in no way a sign that one does not look forward with anticipation to the return of Christ. Indeed, it would be gravely irresponsible for an organization to claim repeatedly that the Second Coming is about to happen and expect its members to make major life choices on that basis. This is precisely what the Watchtower has done, and it is fair to point to this record as an illustration of why one cannot trust one's pastoral care to the organization. The Watchtower itself recognizes this principle:

> Of course, it is easy to say that this group acts as a "prophet" of God. It is another thing to prove it. The only way that this can be done is to review the record. What does it show?[45]

---

[44] *The Watchtower*, 1 December 1984, 18.
[45] Ibid., 1 April 1972, 197.

In the case of the Watchtower, the record shows a string of failed predictions that have left the marital, professional, and spiritual lives of countless Witnesses in ruins as a result of the organization's overzealous proclamations of the Second Coming.

17

Can You Trust
Watchtower Doctrine?

We admit that our organization and its leaders are fallible,[1] and we never claimed to be an inspired prophet.[2] When we make mistakes, we admit them and correct them. True, there have been adjustments and refinements in our teachings, but this is due to successive improvements in our understanding of biblical prophecies and teachings, what we call an "increase of light." This concept is entirely biblical, as Proverbs 4:18 states: "But the path of the righteous ones is like the bright light that is getting lighter and lighter until the day is firmly established." We are growing in our ability to understand God's Word, as Jehovah is still providing direction and scriptural counsel to his people.[3]

Besides erroneous predictions, the Watchtower has misled its members through countless changes in doctrine and practice. Though the Watchtower acknowledges its fallibility and admits its mistakes, one must keep in mind that it has consistently held itself up as God's sole "channel of communication," asserting that it has his constant guidance and direction. If that were true, then whatever doctrines the Watchtower originally taught should still be true today, as truth does not change. But the Watchtower tries to downplay the significance of its doctrinal changes by stating that "matters on which corrections of viewpoint have been needed have been relatively minor when compared with the vital Bible

---

[1] *The Watchtower*, 15 August 1972, 501.

[2] Ibid., 15 May 1976, 297.

[3] Ibid., 1 May 1964, 277.

truths that they have discerned and publicized."[4] In other words, the Witness is supposed to look at the overall picture of the Watchtower organization and see something very positive and reliable, even though there are a few "imperfections" present.

The Watchtower's own history tells quite a different story. An examination of it shows that, not only have minor teachings been altered, but major ones have undergone mutation as well. Listed below are examples of Watchtower doctrines that have clearly been changed or reversed—in some cases asserting the exact opposite of what was once taught.

Again, let us summarize David Reed's compilation of Watchtower reversals.[5]

The Great Crowd

- The great crowd of Revelation 7:9 is not an earthly class but a secondary heavenly class that will be saved to heaven out of the tribulation.[6]

- The great crowd of Revelation 7:9 is an earthly class, not a secondary heavenly class that will be saved to heaven.[7]

Worshiping Christ

- "To worship a false Christ would indeed be sin, but to worship *Christ* in any form cannot be wrong."[8]

---

[4] *Reasoning from the Scriptures* (Brooklyn: Watchtower Bible and Tract Society of New York, 1985), 136–37.

[5] *Index of Watchtower Errors* (Grand Rapids: Baker Book House, 1990).

[6] *Watchtower Reprints*, 458 (*Zion's Watch Tower*, March 1883, 6); 2161 (*Zion's Watch Tower*, 1 June 1897, 161–62); *Jehovah's Witnesses in the Divine Purpose* (Brooklyn: Watchtower Bible and Tract Society of New York, 1959), 140.

[7] *Reasoning from the Scriptures*, 167.

[8] *Watchtower Reprints*, 83 (*Zion's Watch Tower*, March 1880, 4).

- "[I]t is unscriptural for worshippers of the living and true God to render worship to the Son of God, Jesus Christ."[9]

Abaddon

- "Abaddon" of Revelation 9 is "Satan the Devil."[10]

- "Abaddon" of Revelation 9 is "Jesus Christ, the Son of Jehovah God."[11]

Higher Powers

- The "higher powers" or "superior authorities" of Romans 13:1 are "Jehovah God and Christ Jesus," rather than worldly rulers.[12]

- The "higher powers" or "superior authorities" of Romans 13:1 are "secular governmental authorities."[13]

The Men of Sodom

- The men of Sodom will be resurrected.[14]

- The men of Sodom will not be resurrected.[15]

---

[9] *The Watchtower*, 1 November 1964, 671.

[10] *Studies in the Scriptures* (Brooklyn: People's Pulpit Association, 1917), 7:159.

[11] *Then Is Finished the Mystery of God* (Brooklyn: Watchtower Bible and Tract Society of New York, 1969), 232.

[12] *Let God Be True* (Brooklyn: Watchtower Bible and Tract Society of New York, 1952), 248.

[13] *1975 Yearbook of Jehovah's Witnesses* (Brooklyn: Watchtower Bible and Tract Society of New York, 1974), 238.

[14] *Watchtower Reprints*, 7–8 (*Zion's Watch Tower*, July 1879, 7–8).

[15] *The Watchtower*, 1 June 1952, 338.

- The men of Sodom will be resurrected.[16]

- The men of Sodom will not be resurrected.[17]

Military Service

- "Obedience to the laws of the land might at some time oblige us to bear arms, and in such event it would be our duty to go into the army, if unable in any legal and proper manner to obtain exemption, but it would not be our duty to volunteer. . . . There could be nothing against our consciences in going into the army."[18]

- "Notice that there is no command in the Scriptures against military service."[19]

- "It is only due to conscience that they [Witnesses] have personally and legally objected before draft boards to participating in the armed conflicts and defense programs of worldly nations."[20]

- "[T]rue Christians have endeavored to maintain complete neutrality as to conflicts between factions of the world. They do not interfere with what others do about . . . serving in the armed forces. . . . But they themselves worship only Jehovah. . . . [T]hey have dedicated their lives unreservedly to him and give their full support to his Kingdom."[21]

---

[16] Ibid., 1 August 1965, 479.

[17] Ibid., 1 June 1988, 30–31.

[18] *Watchtower Reprints*, 3179–80 (*Zion's Watch Tower*, 15 April 1903, 119–20).

[19] Ibid., 2345 (*Zion's Watch Tower*, 1 August 1898, 231).

[20] *The Watchtower*, 1 February 1951, 73.

[21] *Reasoning from the Scriptures*, 269, 270.

Christmas

- "We may as well join with the civilized world in celebrating the grand event on the day which the majority celebrate— 'Christmas day.' "[22]

- "We all need to face up to the fact that Christmas and its music are not from Jehovah, the God of truth. Then what is their source? Reason should suggest that they are from someone whose sole aim now is to mislead as many people as possible. The Bible tells us that this is the goal of Satan the Devil."[23]

- "A custom that certainly would not be carried on today was the celebration of Christmas with a Christmas tree in the Bethel dining room."[24]

Flags

- "Everyone in America should take pleasure in displaying the American flag."[25]

- "In the colonial days of America the Puritans objected to the British flag because of its red cross of St. George. According to *The Encyclopedia Britannica*, they did this, 'not from any disloyalty to the mother country, but from a conscientious objection to what they deemed an idolatrous symbol.' There are Christians today who feel similarly regarding national flags. They are Jehovah's witnesses. Their position is the same the world over. Being keenly aware of the Scriptural

---

[22] *Watchtower Reprints*, 3468 (*Zion's Watch Tower*, 1 December 1904, 364).

[23] *The Watchtower*, 15 December 1983, 7.

[24] *1975 Yearbook*, 147.

[25] Ibid., 15 May 1917, 6086.

command to 'flee from idolatry,' they decline to participate in flag ceremonies."[26]

Vaccination

- "Vaccination is "a great evil" and "a direct violation of the everlasting covenant God made with Noah."[27]

- "Thinking people would rather have smallpox than vaccination." The practice of vaccinations is "a crime, an outrage, and a delusion."[28]

- "The matter of vaccination is one for the individual that has to face it to decide for himself. . . . After consideration of the matter, it does not appear to us to be in violation of the everlasting covenant made with Noah, as set down in Genesis 9:4, nor contrary to God's related commandment at Leviticus 17:10–14. . . . Hence all objection to vaccination on Scriptural grounds seems to be lacking."[29]

Organ Transplants

- "Those who submit to such operations are thus living off the flesh of another human. That is cannibalistic."[30]

- Organ transplants are not necessarily cannibalistic. They are "a matter of personal decision."[31]

[26] *Awake!*, 8 September 1971, 14.

[27] *Golden Age*, 4 February 1931, 293–94.

[28] Ibid., 1 January 1929.

[29] *The Watchtower*, 15 December 1952, 764.

[30] Ibid., 15 November 1967, 702.

[31] Ibid., 15 March 1980, 31.

Blood Transfusions

- Blood transfusions are unacceptable and cause one to forfeit heaven.[32]

- Blood transfusions are a matter of free choice for Witnesses in Bulgaria. (Jehovah's Witnesses Leadership in Bulgaria, 1999.)[33]

Christ's Return

- Christ returned invisibly in 1874.[34]

- Jesus did not return in 1874 but in 1914.[35]

Peculiar Teachings

In addition to these doctrinal changes, the Watchtower has also promoted some rather peculiar teachings and beliefs. Listed below are a few examples:

- White people living in China eventually produce Chinese offspring—without intermarrying—due to the influence of soil and climate.[36]

---

[32] *Blood, Medicine, and the Law of God* (Brooklyn: Watchtower Bible and Tract Society of New York, 1961), 55.

[33] Secretary to the European Commission of Human Rights, *Information Note No. 148 on the 276th Session of the European Commission of Human Rights* (Strasbourg: European Commission of Human Rights, March 2–Friday 13, 1998). Photocopy in Catholic Answers archives.

[34] *Studies in the Scriptures*, (*The Finished Mystery*), (Brooklyn: People's Pulpit Association, 1917), 7:54, 60, 68.

[35] This is the current Watchtower position.

[36] *Watchtower Reprints*, 3043 (*Zion's Watch Tower*, 15 July 1902, 215–16).

- Jehovah God lives on the star Alcyone in the Pleiades star system, "from which the Almighty governs his universe."[37]

- Jesus is the mediator only for the 144,000, while the anointed remnant is the mediator for the great earthly crowd, since members of this group are not in the New Covenant.[38]

- The mention of "a thousand six hundred furlongs" in Revelation 14:20 is really a reference to the distance between Scranton, Pennsylvania, (where vol. 7 of *Studies in the Scriptures* was written) and the Watchtower headquarters in Brooklyn.[39]

- The Leviathan of Job 40:15–41:34 is a prophecy of a steam locomotive: "Thou wilt lengthen out leviathan [the locomotive] with a hook [automatic coupler] or with a snare [coupling-pin] which thou wilt cause his tongue [coupling-link] to drop down. Wilt thou not place a ring [piston] in his nostrils [cylinder]?"[40]

- "The earlier in the forenoon you take the sun bath, the greater will be the beneficial effect, because you get more of the ultra-violet rays, which are healing."[41]

Downplaying the significance of the changes and peculiar theories, the Watchtower offers Proverbs 4:18 as an explanation of them: "But the path of the righteous ones is like the bright light that is getting lighter and lighter until the day is firmly established." But how can one consider the original falsehoods to be "light" at all?

---

[37] Charles Taze Russell, *Studies in the Scriptures* (Brooklyn: Watchtower Bible and Tract Society, 1891), 3:327; *Reconciliation* (Brooklyn: Watchtower Bible and Tract Society, 1928), 14.

[38] *The Watchtower*, 15 November 1979, 24–27; 1 April 1979, 31.

[39] *Studies in the Scriptures*, (*The Finished Mystery*), (Brooklyn: People's Pulpit Association, 1917), 7:230.

[40] Ibid., 85.

[41] *Golden Age*, 13 September 1933, 777.

When pressed further on the matter, the Watchtower published an illustration to help explain the changes. It explained that these corrections "might be compared to what is known in navigational circles as 'tacking.' By maneuvering the sails the sailors can cause a ship to go from right to left, back and forth, but all the time making progress toward their destination in spite of contrary winds."[42]

In Ephesians 4:13–14, the Watchtower claimed, Paul speaks of something similar—acquiring "accurate knowledge" and encouraging the faithful to "no longer be babes, tossed about as by waves and carried hither and thither by every wind of teaching by means of the trickery of men, by means of cunning and contriving error." But rather than heed St. Paul's admonition, the Witnesses are told to "move ahead with Jehovah's organization"[43]—even in spite of the changes and contradictions—and to view these "adjustments" as opportunities to demonstrate loyalty to the Watchtower:

> Actually, any adjustments that have been made in understanding have furnished an opportunity for those being served by this "slave" to show loyalty and love, the kind of love that Jesus said would mark his followers. . . . For those who truly love God's law there is no stumbling block.[44]

So if an honest Witness finds it a "stumbling block" that the Watchtower has contradicted so many of its prior teachings, that Witness is challenged to be loyal, or to "truly love God's law," by essentially ignoring those contradictions or writing them off as "old light." But the concept of "old light" was addressed by Charles Taze Russell when the Watchtower sect was still in its infancy and before it altered any of its doctrines. In fact, Russell pointed to this very concept as one of the flaws of the Adventist sect he left behind:

---

[42] *The Watchtower*, 1 December 1981, 27. The text is accompanied by a drawing of a sailboat making a zigzag path, the net effect of which is a forward direction.

[43] Ibid., 1 June 1967, 335.

[44] Ibid., 1 March 1979, 24.

If we were following a man undoubtedly it would be different with us; undoubtedly one human idea would contradict another and that which was light one or two or six years ago would be regarded as darkness now; But with God there is no variableness, neither shadow of turning, and so it is with truth; any knowledge or light coming from God must be like its author. A new view of truth never can contradict a former truth. "New light" never extinguishes older "light," but adds to it. If you were lighting up a building containing seven gas jets you would not extinguish one every time you lighted another, but would add one light to another and they would be in harmony and thus give increase of light: So it is with the light of truth; the true increase is by adding to, not by substituting one for another. [45]

The Watchtower still maintains that Jesus approved its "accurate" teachings back in 1918. But what was the Watchtower teaching then? It had just published *Studies in the Scriptures*, vol. 7 (*The Finished Mystery*), in 1917, and it taught, among other things, that Jesus had returned in 1874, that God would destroy all of Christendom's churches by 1918 (killing millions in the process), that the "little flock" of Bible students would be glorified in 1918, and that God's kingdom would be established in 1931. [46]

Since these teachings proved to be false, which the Watchtower admits, why would Jesus have considered an organization disseminating such doctrines to be "providing spiritual food"? Surely Jesus would have known that these teachings were untrue. If Jesus did give his approval to such beliefs, then the Watchtower would no longer have God's favor for having since rejected them.

This brief list of contradictions will, one hopes, illustrate to the sincere Witness that the Watchtower is an inconsistent and misleading organization and, thus, unworthy of trust. The Witness has no certainty that what he is being taught today by the Watchtower will not be rejected in another twenty, thirty, or fifty years as "apostate doctrines of men," or "old light," as the organization

---

[45] *Watchtower Reprints*, 188 (*Zion's Watch Tower*, February 1881), 3.

[46] Leonard and Marjorie Chretien, *Witnesses of Jehovah* (Eugene, Oregon: Harvest House, 1988), 64.

sometimes calls it. A much longer list of scriptural contradictions and doctrinal twists could be formulated,[47] but the above examples suffice to remove any reason one might have to believe that "it is through the columns of *The Watchtower* that Jehovah provides direction and constant Scriptural counsel to his people."[48] God is not the author of error and contradiction, so the explanation for such mistakes and mutations is that the Watchtower does *not* speak for God.

---

[47] See David Reed, ed., *Index of Watchtower Errors* (Grand Rapids: Baker Book House, 1990).

[48] *The Watchtower*, 1 May 1964, 277.

18

Was There a Great Apostasy?

In 2 Thessalonians 2:3, Paul states that the day of Jehovah "will not come unless the apostasy comes first and the man of lawlessness gets revealed, the son of destruction." So, even within the lifetime of the apostles, there were wolves in sheeps' clothing in the Christian congregation. These spread their false teachings, and by the time the apostles had died, the apostasy was well under way. Thus, the pure message of Jehovah was buried under the doctrines of men and pagan philosophy until God appointed his faithful servant, the Watchtower, to reclaim the ancient truths. Today, some claim to believe the Bible but reject Jehovah's organization. They, too, are apostates.[1]

The theory of a great apostasy among the early Christians is common among certain groups, such as Mormons and Jehovah's Witnesses, that lack historical roots. In the latter case, since there are no historical documents showing their existence or the body of their teachings prior to the nineteenth century, the Watchtower is left to conclude that apostates must have destroyed all of the records in the first centuries. In reading the Church Fathers, one finds a great sensitivity, even scrupulosity, to keep the apostolic teaching untainted by the philosophies and novel teachings of men. At the slightest infringement on the truth taught by Christ, the early Christian writers vociferously protested. The early-Church historian will see, not a gradual descent into pagan deception, but a clearly marked battle between Christ's Church and any number

---

[1] *Reasoning from the Scriptures* (Brooklyn: Watchtower Bible and Tract Society of New York, 1985), 34–37.

of heresies that attacked it. G. K. Chesterton beautifully expresses the drama:

> It is always simple to fall; there are an infinity of angles at which one falls, only one at which one stands. To have fallen into any one of the fads from Gnosticism to Christian Science would indeed have been obvious and tame. But to have avoided them all has been one whirling adventure; and in my vision the heavenly chariot flies thundering through the ages, the dull heresies sprawling and prostrate.[2]

There are at least three practical problems with the concept of a great apostasy. For one, it makes Jesus look like the foolish builder he describes in Matthew 7:26–27. The fool built his house on sand, and it collapsed. If Wisdom Incarnate founded the Church as a house built upon a rock (1 Tim. 3:15; Matt. 16:18), should one expect it to share the fate of the house built by the fool on sand? "And the rain poured down and the floods came and the winds blew and struck against that house and it caved in, and its collapse was great" (Matt. 7:27). If the Church had collapsed less than a century after Christ, then he did not keep his promise of the gates of hell never prevailing against it (Matt. 16:18).

Secondly, the idea of an immediate and widespread apostasy argues against the divine institution of Christianity. In Acts 5, for instance, the great rabbi Gamaliel spoke thus to the Jewish leaders in regard to the apostles and the reality of their teaching if it came from God:

> "Men of Israel, pay attention to yourselves as to what YOU intend to do respecting these men. For instance, before these days Theu'das rose, saying he himself was somebody, and a number of men, about four hundred, joined his party. But he was done away with, and all those who were obeying him were dispersed and came to nothing. After him Judas the Galilean rose in the days of the registration, and he drew off people after him. And yet that man perished, and all those who were obeying him were scattered abroad. And so, under the present circumstances, I say to you, do not meddle with

---

[2] G. K. Chesterton, *Orthodoxy* (New York: Image/Doubleday, 1990), 101.

these men, but let them alone; (because if this scheme is or this work is of men, it will be overthrown; but if it is from God, you will not be able to overthrow them)." (Acts 5:35–39)

There is but one Church that has not been overthrown since the time of Christ—the Catholic Church. If there had been a small congregation of Christians that held to Watchtower doctrines in apostolic times, then by the Watchtower's own admission they were overthrown, dispersed, and came to nothing. According to Acts 5, any organization that was present at the time of Christ and disappeared for over eighteen hundred years (which is essentially what the Watchtower claims) is not the work of God but of men.

The more a Witness affirms that the Church apostatized within a few centuries, the more he digs a hole for himself. He will assert that by the time of Constantine (c. A.D. 313), the Church had essentially become a gang of neo-pagan political-idol worshipers. One difficulty with this is that this same group of "apostates" selected the books of the Bible in the year 382 at the Council of Rome. The Catholic Church's determination of the biblical canon was based upon those writings that were in accordance with apostolic Tradition. A writing that did not square with the doctrines of the apostles as they were passed on through the Church's teaching authority could not have been inspired. So the Witness is left with an "apostate" body of fourth-century Catholic bishops selecting the New Testament canon used in Kingdom Halls each week. If the Witness denies the teaching authority of the Catholic Church, he is therefore left with a fallible collection of books for which he cannot prove inspiration.

19

How Do You Witness
to the Witnesses?

Whenever you have an opportunity to speak with Witnesses, the first step is to make use of it. When that knock on the door comes, don't turn off the lights and hide. Even if you don't wish to speak with them, take all of the literature they offer you. If you don't wish to read it, fine. Just throw it away. If you refuse it, it will find its way into other people's hands—and possibly result in the loss of a soul. By taking as much as they give you, you are keeping others from reading it. (If you do take the literature, the Witnesses are more likely to return. Don't worry. Just accept more magazines the next time. In the meantime, you may want to prepare yourself to discuss the material with the Witnesses.)

It is also important to recognize when circumstances do not permit us to evangelize. If we are weak in our own faith or do not have the time or resources needed to rebut the objections that Witnesses would confront us with, then our own spiritual good would incline us not to engage Witnesses in dialogue. However, if you've read this book this far, you are probably well situated to share the gospel with Witnesses and to deflect the charges they will make.

When you do speak with Witnesses, realize that quite a large percentage of them are either ex-Catholics or have a strong bias against the Church. They have read countless pages of Watchtower material attacking Catholicism, so they will see you as someone who worships statues of Mary, communicates with the dead, and thinks that professing faith in three gods is biblical. In the face of such grave misunderstandings, remain calm and charitable. Show them great kindness, since they expect to be "persecuted." Each time they feel that they are being persecuted, they take it as evidence that they are doing the work of God, so keep in mind Paul's words: "A slave of the Lord should not quarrel, but should be gentle with everyone, able to teach, tolerant, correcting opponents with kindness" (2 Tim. 2:24–25; NAB).

Do not be threatening, intimidating, or pushy—you do not want to give them a reason to leave. They expect hostility; they must be met with hospitality. You cannot hope to change people unless you love them—and they know that you love them. This approach cannot be overemphasized. Even if Witnesses totally disagree with your theology, they will not forget the kindness, respect, and Christian charity you show them—and this may be the starting place for them to turn from the Watchtower organization and embrace the truth of the Catholic faith.

During your conversations, do not make your arguments personal by saying, "Why do you believe so and so?" or even "Why do Jehovah's Witnesses teach such and such?" Rather, focus all arguments on the Watchtower organization, not on its members. The Witness will be less defensive, since your approach will not be seen as a personal attack. (In a sense, you want to create a "you and I versus the Watchtower" approach.)

To avoid appearing confrontational, use questions as your arguments. This is very helpful when dealing with people who do not expect to learn from you. It is especially relevant with the Witnesses because they are at your doorstep with the intent to instruct *you*. If you become overbearing or confrontational in your dealings with them, however, you will be perceived as "an opposer"—this is the Watchtower term—and they will seek to end the conversation.

Though a Witness may wish to lead a conversation by explaining to you how the Trinity is a pagan and unbiblical concept, don't take the bait and enter into a winding discussion, slinging verses back and forth, taking a long time and getting nowhere. For the Witness even to begin considering the truth of the Trinity, he needs to accept that the Watchtower might be wrong, that Jesus and the Holy Spirit are both God, and that what seems to him to be a mysterious, pagan, philosophical, three-headed god is actually the Jehovah God he wishes to serve.

The Witnesses are well trained in how to deflect arguments concerning the Trinity. For this reason it is wise to begin with a more useful topic, namely the issue of authority—whose should be trusted and why—and later come back to the subject of the Trinity. It is a matter of authority. Will they accept you—a Trinitarian apostate—to provide them with a true interpretation over and against the Watchtower, which is "Jehovah's organization"? Not until they have learned to see the Watchtower for what it is rather than what it claims to be. You must focus on the Watchtower organization's lack of credibility. Then the doctrines will fall with it.

The above chapter on the reliability of the Watchtower will be useful in explaining to them why *you* cannot trust the Watchtower—and why *they* shouldn't, either. Many people look into becoming Witnesses because of the friendly nature of the Witnesses they meet and because they have never been invited to study the Bible before. Odds are, they never studied it with someone other than Witnesses and really know no other authority. Witnesses can sound convincing to those who are not familiar with the issues and do not know how to respond to them.

Once the issue of authority has been covered and you wish to deal with specific doctrines, you should begin with those that are more difficult for Witnesses to support, such as the idea that Jesus is Michael the archangel. Where does the Bible clearly teach this? Make sure that they are not spending the time trying to debunk the Catholic teaching but building a case for their own. Ask for verses showing that Michael created the universe or has the power to forgive sins.

Keep in mind one key point when talking with a Witness: They are notorious for changing the subject whenever they see themselves being backed into a theological corner or discussing a topic that is problematic for their belief system. (They have learned by example at Kingdom Hall meetings to do this, although they generally are not fully aware that they do it.) Whatever you do, keep the conversation *on track* and on *one* subject at a time. If he raises another issue, respond by saying, "That's an interesting topic, and I'd like very much to discuss it, but since we're currently discussing *this* topic, can we save the other subject for another time? Perhaps we can talk about that issue during your next visit." With such a statement from you, you simultaneously keep the discussion focused and schedule a future visit!

Witnesses are told to avoid people who wish to convert them, and if you come off as an opposer, they will not allow you to offer a laundry list of tough questions. They will be eager to teach but slow to listen. So take advantage of this, instead of expecting them to sit and learn from you. For example, instead of saying, "Your doctrine on the patriarchs' not going to heaven is wrong because of Matthew 8:11," say, "I read that material you gave me, and there were some things I really agreed with. But it said that none of the patriarchs went to heaven, and I always thought that they did. Maybe I didn't understand your position clearly, but I read this in Matthew 8:11. . . . What does your translation say?"

If you only have a moment to speak with them, verses such as Matthew 8:11 and John 2:18–21—where Jesus predicts the resurrection of his body—are useful to ask them to study and pray about, since they are such blatant contradictions of Watchtower teaching. Have them read aloud to you the verses from their own translation, since they will be less influenced by listening to you read it from yours.

You may need to play the student in order to talk a Witness into taking any information from you. For example you might say, "These few pages of arguments I found [give him a tract, or pages from this book] make it very difficult for me to consider becoming a Jehovah's Witness, since it appears that your beliefs are unbiblical. If I were convinced that the Watchtower is right, I'd join, because I need to be honest with God. I'll read your *Awake!* and *Watchtower* magazines, and perhaps you could work through this to give me the Witness angle on it all, showing where is it is off the mark, misrepresenting you, etc., and then we'll meet here next week to discuss both."

Don't jump from topic to topic, and make sure that passages are read in context! If the Witness tosses out twenty-five objections against the Church, take the one you feel most confident in answering and stick with it. Leave a topic alone if you feel you aren't getting the point across. Never attempt to make the Witness admit to you that he is wrong, but let your words germinate in his mind and heart.

At some point during the conversation, inquire if the Witness was once Catholic, and, if so, why he left. Sincerely ask what the Lord has done in his life. This will open his heart, and to the extent that you are a good listener, he will be more prone to listen in return. As the Scriptures command, "Before hearing, answer not, and interrupt no one in the middle of his speech. . . . Prepare your words and you will be listened to; draw upon your training, and then give your answer" (Sir. 8:8; 33:4; NAB). In response to his answer, share your testimony and love for the Catholic faith.

When you present this to him, he may respond with a storm of objections to the Catholic faith. Be open to discussing any problems that he may have, and if you feel unprepared to answer any of his questions, fine! Let him know that you aren't sure how to answer but would like to research a bit and meet in a week to share what you find. Your humility will go a long way to open his heart.

Some people refuse to admit when they do not know an answer, and they attempt to save face by either changing the subject or making up an answer that they are not sure of. It's better to decline to answer until you've done your homework.[1] So prepare yourself to give a reason for the hope that is in you (1 Pet. 3:15), and begin to read the Scriptures daily if you do not do so already.

Always realize the delicacy of the conversion of a Witness. It

---

[1] Some good resources for defending the faith include Karl Keating's book *Catholicism and Fundamentalism* (San Francisco: Ignatius Press, 1988) and the websites *www.catholic.com* and *www.jamesakin.com*.

is not simply a matter of a person's switching doctrinal positions but of reordering his entire life. Converting to Catholicism would mean being exiled from friends and any family members who are still Witnesses. There is a tremendous amount of his life that has been invested in being a member of the organization. So patience, sensitivity, and love must be present in all your conversations with a Witness. Let him set the pace at which he ingests the information you present to him. When working to get someone out of the Watchtower, make sure to provide a loving alternative, a community that will accept him. This will make the transition more realistic—and less daunting.

As in all efforts of evangelism, lead him ever closer to Christ. Remind him that the Watchtower is not his Savior. Ask him to read the Bible more than *The Watchtower*. The average Witness is assigned to read three thousand pages of Watchtower literature each year, compared to less than two hundred pages of Scripture.[2] Suggest that he do the opposite: Read through the Bible twice a year, and read no more than two hundred pages of the Watchtower. After all, God is the author of one, and it has no mistakes. Watchtower literature, on the contrary, is written by fallible men and contains many errors, some of which it has admitted in print.

The sooner you witness to a Witness, the better. It is easy to sway someone who has only begun looking into the Witnesses by exposing him to the real history of the Watchtower. But once he has been given a few Bible studies, he'll be warned that others will try to stop the study:

> How might Satan use friends and relatives to discourage us? . . . You can be sure that the Devil does not want you to have this knowledge, and that he will do all in his power to stop you from getting it. . . . But if you give up a study of God's Word when opposition comes, how will God view you?[3]

---

[2] David Reed, *How to Rescue Your Loved One From the Watchtower* (Grand Rapids: Baker Book House, 1991), 9.

[3] *You Can Live Forever in Paradise on Earth* (Brooklyn: Watchtower Bible and Tract Society of New York, 1982), 23–24.

If you oppose his study, the Watchtower will appear as a prophet, and you'll be seen as an instrument of the devil. If the person you are trying to reach has been involved in the organization for a long period of time, be especially patient and prayerful. God desires his conversion more than you do. See God's mercy and patience as an example to follow.

Do not be discouraged if you do not see instantaneous conversions. Consider Eutychus in Acts 20:9. While Paul was preaching the gospel to him, Eutychus dozed off, fell out of a window, and plummeted to his death! If the finest of apostolic preaching can end in such disaster, we have no grounds for discouragement when we don't see instant conversions. It is the Holy Spirit who brings about any conversion, so pray for Witnesses individually and as a group. In the meantime, know that "neither the one who plants nor the one who waters is anything, but only God, who causes the growth" (1 Cor. 3:7; NAB).

Do not judge the success of a conversation by how many verses you quoted, or the failure of a discussion by how little the other seemed to be swayed. No changes will take place without grace. For that reason, your efforts in prayer are of preeminent importance. Pray before, during, and after conversations. You may entirely botch a conversation with a Witness but win his soul by fervent prayers offered long after your meeting.

Lastly, never neglect your own continual conversion to Christ. It is very easy to see others as projects—entirely forgetting the spiritual work that should be done on oneself. As soon as you realize and desire your own continual interior conversion of heart more than the conversion of a Witness, you will win souls for Christ. As St. John Vianney said, "What will convert [others] will be the sanctity of your own life!"[4]

May all of the holy angels and saints, the Queen of Apostles, and the glorious Trinity abundantly bless your evangelization.

---

[4] *Thoughts of the Curé D'Ars* (Rockford, Illinois: TAN Books and Publishers, 1984), 16.